**Illinois Central College
Learning Resource Center**

# THE PHOENIX

Illustrations of the phoenix from Bestiaries

*Above* MS. C.C.C.C. 53 fol. 200b : *left* the phoenix in a ball of spices looks at the sun ; *right* the phoenix lies dead in the ball, and a little winged dragon which will become the new phoenix flies away.
*Below* MS. Royal 12 C XIX fol. 49b : *left* the phoenix plucks twigs from a tree ; *right* the phoenix is immolated on an altar.

OLD AND MIDDLE ENGLISH TEXTS

*General Editor :* G. L. BROOK

# The Phoenix

*Edited by*

N. F. BLAKE

MANCHESTER
UNIVERSITY PRESS

PRINTED BY R. & R. CLARK, LTD., EDINBURGH

# PREFACE

BECAUSE of high printing costs, modern editions of Old English texts can never be as comprehensive as their editors would wish. Consequently in this edition of *The Phoenix* I have attempted to provide students and scholars with a sound text together with such comment as is necessary for an understanding of the poem and its background. It has not, however, been possible to reproduce all the theories which have been put forward about the poem and particular passages in it. Similarly it has been impossible to include complete references in the glossaries. Nevertheless I have decided to add in appendices the two Latin sources of the Old English poem and the prose versions of the phoenix story in Old English and Old Icelandic so that the poem can be placed in its West European background and so that the poet's achievement can be more readily evaluated by a comparison of the various accounts, which are here gathered together in one book for the first time.

I should like to thank the Librarian of Corpus Christi College, Cambridge, for permission to reprint the illustration from MS. C.C.C.C. 53 fol. 200b ; the Trustees of the British Museum for permission to reprint the illustration from MS. Royal 12 C XIX fol. 49b; Hölder-Pichler-Tempsky Verlagsbuchhandlung, Vienna, for permission to reprint the passage from Ambrose's *Hexameron* from *Corpus Scriptorum Ecclesiasticorum Latinorum*, vol. 32, pars 1 (1896), pp. 197-8 ; B. G. Teubner Verlagsgesellschaft, Leipzig, for permission to reprint the *Carmen de ave phoenice* from A. Riese's *Anthologia Latina*, pars prior (1906), No. 485a. The texts of the Old English and Old Icelandic prose versions are based on manuscripts in the British Museum and Det Arnamagnæanske Institut, Copenhagen, respectively and I should like to thank these institutions for putting these manuscripts at my disposal. The text of *The Phoenix* is based on the facsimile edition of *The Exeter Book* (1933). I should like to thank the Librarian

of the Society of Antiquaries of London for permission to
see the Douce bequest. I have also had the privilege of
working in several other libraries in the course of the pre-
paration of this book, but I should particularly like to
thank the staff of the Harold Cohen Library in the University of Liverpool for answering my queries and carrying
out my requests so promptly and courteously.

I am greatly indebted to many of my colleagues in
Liverpool who have willingly helped me with many details
of the phoenix myth, such as the Egyptian and Greek
accounts. Their assistance made my task easier and I
thank them for it. I should like to extend my warmest
thanks to Professor Simeon Potter who has followed the
progress of the edition with interest and who has made
comments and suggestions at all stages. The edition owes
much to his kindly help and penetrating criticism. Professor Brook likewise read through the typescript and the
proofs, and he has suggested many improvements. I should
like to thank him not only for that, but also for all the
advice he has offered me in his rôle of general editor.
Finally I should like to thank Miss M. Burton for typing
out my draft copy so accurately.

N. BLAKE

Liverpool, 1963

# CONTENTS

# ABBREVIATIONS

| | |
|---|---|
| *AB* | *Anglia Beiblatt* |
| *BBA* | *Bonner Beiträge zur Anglistik* |
| *Beitr.* | *Beiträge zur Geschichte der deutschen Sprache und Literatur*, edited by H. Paul and W. Braune |
| Blake | N. F. Blake, 'Some Problems of Interpretation and Translation in the OE *Phoenix*', *Anglia*, lxxx (1962), 50-62 |
| Bright | J. W. Bright, *An Anglo-Saxon Reader*. New York, 1891 |
| BT | *An Anglo-Saxon Dictionary* based on the manuscript collections of the late J. Bosworth, edited and enlarged by T. N. Toller. With Supplement by T. N. Toller. Oxford, 1898–1921 |
| Campbell | A. Campbell, *Old English Grammar*. Oxford, 1959 |
| *Carmen* | *Carmen de ave phoenice* (Appendix I (a)) |
| Cook | A. S. Cook, *The Old English Elene, Phoenix, and Physiologus*. New Haven, 1919 |
| EETS | Early English Text Society |
| Emerson | O. F. Emerson, 'Originality in Old English Poetry', *RES*, ii (1926), 18-31 |
| Ettmüller | L. Ettmüller, *Engla and Seaxna Scôpas and Bôceras*. Quedlinburg and Leipzig, 1850 |
| Fitzpatrick | M. C. Fitzpatrick, *Lactanti de ave phoenice*. Diss. Philadelphia, 1933 |
| Gollancz | I. Gollancz, *The Exeter Book*, part I. EETS Original Series 104. London, 1895 |
| Grein | C. W. M. Grein, *Bibliothek der angelsächsischen Poesie*, vol. I. Göttingen, 1857 |

| | |
|---|---|
| Grundtvig | N. F. S. Grundtvig, *Phenix-Fuglen, et angelsachsisk Kvad.* Copenhagen, 1840 |
| Hall | J. L. Hall, *Judith, Phoenix, and other Anglo-Saxon Poems.* New York, 1902 |
| *JEGP* | *Journal of English and Germanic Philology* |
| Kennedy | C. W. Kennedy, *The Poems of Cynewulf.* London, 1910 |
| Krapp-Dobbie | *The Exeter Book*, edited by G. P. Krapp and E. v. K. Dobbie. New York, 1936 |
| MHG | Middle High German |
| *MLN* | *Modern Language Notes* |
| *NQ* | *Notes and Queries* |
| OE | Old English |
| OED | *The Oxford English Dictionary* |
| OHG | Old High German |
| ON | Old Norse |
| Orosius | *King Alfred's Orosius*, part I, edited by H. Sweet. EETS Original Series 79. London, 1883 |
| *Pat. Gr.* | *Patrologia Græca*, edited by J.-P. Migne |
| *Pat. Lat.* | *Patrologia Latina*, edited by J.-P. Migne |
| *PMLA* | *Publications of the Modern Language Association of America* |
| *PP* | *The Prose Phoenix* (Appendix II (a)) |
| *RES* | *Review of English Studies* |
| Schlemilch | W. Schlemilch, 'Beiträge zur Sprache und Orthographie spätaltengl. Sprachdenkmäler der Übergangszeit (1000–1150)', *Stud.*, xxxiv (1914) |
| Schlotterose | O. Schlotterose, 'Die altenglische Dichtung "Phoenix"', *BBA*, xxv (1908) |
| Sievers-Brunner | *Altenglische Grammatik nach der Angelsächsischen Grammatik von E. Sievers*, revised by K. Brunner. 2nd edition. Halle, 1951 |

*Stud.*              *Studien zur englischen Philologie*, ed. L. Morsbach, Halle

Sweet              H. Sweet, *An Anglo-Saxon Reader*. Oxford, 1876

Thorpe            B. Thorpe, *Codex Exoniensis*. London, 1842

# INTRODUCTION

## THE MANUSCRIPT

THE Old English poem *The Phoenix* is found in the poetic codex known as the Exeter Book, which is now in the library of Exeter Cathedral. It has been there at least since 1072, for a book described as *·i· mycel Englisc bōc be gehwilcum þingum on lēoðwīsan geworht*, which is usually understood to refer to the Exeter Book, is found listed among the donations of Bishop Leofric. This Leofric became Bishop of Devon and Cornwall in 1046. He was confirmed in his bishopric by William the Conqueror and he died in 1072, about which time the list of his donations was made.

A facsimile of the Exeter Book together with an account of its history and palaeography was edited in 1933 by R. W. Chambers, M. Förster and R. Flower, where a full description of the codex can be found. *The Phoenix* is written on folios 55b-65b. The handwriting is clearly legible and reading the text presents no difficulty. Only a few points about the manuscript which concern the text printed here need be mentioned. Accents are used in the codex, but they have not been retained in the text.[1] The few abbreviations that occur, e.g. *þon* (*þonne* 31) and *wundrū* (*wundrum* 63), have been expanded silently. The ampersand has been expanded to *ond*, as *a* plus nasal is represented by *o* in the Exeter Book. The characters ȝ and *wynn* have been modernised to *g* and *w* respectively. Compound words, the elements of which are often written separately in the manuscript, are written as one word in the text. The scribe has divided the poem into eight sections (1-84, 85-181, 182-264, 265-349, 350-423, 424-517, 518-88 and 589-677) by the use of capital letters at the beginning of each section. This division into sections has not, however, been retained in this edition. It might also be noted

---

[1] A list of these may be found in Krapp-Dobbie, pp. lxxxii ff.

here that certain graphic lapses are characteristic of the scribe of the Exeter Book, such as the writing of *f* for *s* (cf. line 15) and of *w* for *þ* (cf. line 115). The occurrence of similar mistakes throughout the Exeter Book makes the emendations at these places almost certain.[1] There are a number of corrections in the Exeter Book made by the scribe himself, which, as we shall see in the next section, tend to make the language more uniform and conceal the developments taking place in the language. But one correction, which does not fall into this class, can perhaps be noted here. Twice in *The Phoenix* (lines 327, 584), but nowhere else in the Exeter Book, *n* is corrected by the scribe to *þ*.

The Exeter Book differs from the other three poetic codices in that it is a poetic miscellany in which there does not appear to have been a recognisable principle of selection. The earlier part contains lengthy religious poems, the latter shorter poems, both secular and religious. On palaeographical grounds the codex has been dated to *c.* 970–90.[2] But Dr. Sisam has drawn attention to the stately, even style of the writing and he concluded from this that the scribe of the Exeter Book was copying from an anthology which was already in existence.[3] Because the codex shows a surprising conformity in language, it must have been copied by a succession of scribes who were not only able, but also regarded themselves as free to standardise the spelling of the manuscript they were copying. Dr. Sisam has shown that this kind of free copying is more characteristic of the early half of the ninth century and he suggested that the original compilation was made in the time of Alfred, Edward or Athelstan.[4]

---

[1] Cf. *Crist*, 31, 133, 306, 371, etc.

[2] R. Flower, 'The script of the Exeter Book', *The Exeter Book of Old English Poetry*, ed. R. W. Chambers, M. Förster, R. Flower, 1933, p. 90.

[3] K. Sisam, *Studies in the History of Old English Literature*, 1953, pp. 97 ff. See also N. Blake, 'The Scribe of the Exeter Book', *Neophilologus*, xlvi (1962), 316-19.

[4] *Op. cit.*, pp. 107-8.

## LANGUAGE

It is generally agreed that the Exeter Book was written by one scribe throughout.[1] It differs from the other poetic codices, which reveal variations in dialect between one poem or group of poems and another, in that there is a strong tendency to linguistic conformity. Examples of the distinctive characteristics which appear in all parts of the Exeter Book have been listed by Dr. Sisam [2] and those which appear in *The Phoenix* can be briefly listed here :

(i) Short *o* appears in stressed syllables before nasals almost regularly : e.g. *mongum* 4, *lond* 20, *monnes* 128. The exceptions are *swanes* 137, *scancan* 310, *gehwane* 464.

(ii) The form of the pronoun *hīe* is almost always *hī* or *hȳ*, e.g. 247, 327, 389, etc.

(iii) The characteristic WS *ie*, especially in the group *gie-*, is more common in the Exeter Book than in the other codices, e.g. 461, 571, etc.

Dr. Sisam noted furthermore that the scribe of the Exeter Book shows all the signs of being a slavish copyist and consequently it is unlikely that he is responsible for the conformity of the language. The poems had certainly been gathered together into an anthology some considerable time before the Exeter Book itself was written. *The Phoenix*, like the other poems in the codex, is written in a standardised West Saxon dialect and the standardisation of the language of the poems in the anthology was probably started at a relatively early date in the anthology's history. But although the bulk of the linguistic forms can be ascribed to the late West Saxon dialect, there are other forms which might be described as Anglian, e.g. *caldum* 59, or Kentish, e.g. *gefreogum* 29. Yet it cannot be proved from these forms that the poem was originally written in an Anglian or even

---

[1] Flower (*op. cit.*, p. 83) suggested that there were several hands in the Exeter Book, but Sisam (*op. cit.*, p. 97) rejected this. It is now generally agreed that there is only one hand, cf. N. R. Ker, *Catalogue of Manuscripts containing Anglo-Saxon*, 1957, No. 116.

[2] *Op. cit.*, pp. 100 ff.

a Kentish dialect, which later West Saxon scribes have attempted to transform into standard West Saxon. It is quite possible that there was in existence in Old English times a poetic language which was not closely related to any of the major dialects, but which contained elements otherwise characteristic of these dialects. The original poem might have been composed in this poetic language and thus it would be impossible to determine in what geographical area the poem was written. But quite apart from the possibility of this poetic language, few Old English dialects ever achieved a standard orthography. Early West Saxon texts, for example, contain many forms which are normally associated with the Anglian dialect. An investigation into the dialect of the poem would hardly lead to any firm conclusions as to the dialect in which the poem was originally composed and consequently an investigation of this sort has not been included here.[1]

Recently dissatisfaction has been expressed at the older system of editing the Old English poetic texts, by which many forms which we now know to be characteristic of late Old English were emended out of existence.[2] Thus *rēmig* (126) is generally emended by editors to *hrēmig*, even though it is well known that there is a tendency for initial *h* to fall in the group *hr-* in late Old English. It is interesting that the very earliest editors did not emend the language so much as later editors have done, and both Grundtvig and Thorpe read *rēmig* here. Emendations of this sort, which appear commonly in most editions of the poetic texts, are not the result of an unintelligible text, but represent an attempt to standardise the language. But it has never been clear in the past what standard was being applied and previous editors have not agreed as to how much ought to

[1] The language has been investigated by H. Bauer, *Ueber die Sprache und Mundart der altenglischen Dichtungen Andreas, Gûðlâc, Phönix, hl. Kreuz und Höllenfahrt Christi,* 1890. There is also a brief investigation in Schlotterose, pp. 69 ff., which is designed to support his view that the poem was written in Northumbria.

[2] G. L. Brook, 'The relation between the textual and linguistic study of Old English', *The Anglo-Saxons,* ed. P. Clemoes, 1959, pp. 280-91.

be emended in this way.[1] Since both the date and the dialect of the original poem are uncertain, it is not possible to edit the poem in the language of its composer. No editor has in fact attempted this. But the poems the scribe was copying were written in a standardised language, which the scribe attempted to reproduce. This seems clear, for there are many corrections made by the scribe in the manuscript which reflect a tendency towards conformity. Most of the forms emended by the editors are variants from this standard, and it could be suggested that if the non-standard forms had been pointed out to the scribe, he might well have altered them in the manuscript. Yet these are not sufficient grounds for emending the text. The standardised language in the codex is not by any means uniform, and we cannot always tell now what variant spellings were tolerated then. Scholars are never likely therefore to achieve a commonly accepted text. Furthermore these forms, as Professor Brook pointed out, are extremely valuable in determining the development of language and orthography in the tenth century. As spelling variants are generally preserved in modern editions of the Old English prose texts, it would seem sensible and helpful to the student to bring the poetic texts into line with them. The language of the poems could then more easily be compared with the prose texts of the transition period from Old to Middle English, which are full of many similar variant spellings. Consequently in this edition the variant forms have been preserved in the text, though they have usually been pointed out in the notes and the glossary. Nevertheless I have considered it desirable to include a list of the more important ones here.

## A. *Vowels in Stressed Syllables*

(i) Confusion of *eo* and *o*, especially in the group *weo-* : *weordum* 425. Schlemilch found the writing of *eo* for *o*

---

[1] I am not here concerned with those suggestions that have been made that all poetic texts should be converted into an artificial standardised language, such as F. P. Magoun Jnr.'s 'A Brief Plea

fairly common in late Old English texts and suggested that as it occurs most frequently in the group *weo-* it was a reverse spelling arising from the change of *weo-* to *wo*.[1]

(ii) Confusion of *eo* and *ea* : *gefēon* 248, and also at *Crist* 1294. Although the confusion of *eo* and *ea* is regarded as characteristic of the Northumbrian dialect in the earlier Old English period, it is found generally in many late Old English texts.[2]

## B.  *Vowels in Unstressed Syllables*

(i) The gradual weakening of the vowels in the final unstressed syllables to the *schwa* sound with the consequent confusion of the various vowels in writing has been thoroughly investigated already.[3]  The following examples are found in *The Phoenix* : *hrēosað* for *hrēoseð* 60, *heoredrēorges* for *heorodrēorges* 217, *sendað* for *sendeð* 488, *lǣdaþ* for *lǣded* 491, *āstellað* for *āstelleð* 511, *hearde* for *hearda* 613. It is possible that *hěrra* 28 which some editors emend to *hěrre* should be included here, and the form *weorþeð* 240, which is corrected in the manuscript from *weorþað*, should also be noted.

(ii) The loss of a medial unstressed vowel occurs at *fægran* 330, which most editors emend to *fægerran*. But syncopy of the medial vowel is common, cp. *gecornum* 388, as is simplification of double consonants. The form *fægran* is also found at *Orosius*, p. 216.

## C.  *Consonants*

(i) Fall of initial *h* :

(a) *h* + liquid : *rēmig* 126, *swēglēoþres* 137. This change is found frequently in the later Nor-

---

for a Normalization of Old-English Poetical Texts', *Les Langues Modernes*, xlv (1951), 63-9.

[1] Schlemilch, p. 15.          [2] Schlemilch, pp. 26, 32, 36.

[3] K. Malone, 'When did Middle English begin ?', *Curme Volume of Linguistic Studies* (*Language Monograph*, No. 7, 1930), 110-17, and A. H. Marckwardt, 'Verb Inflections in Late Old English', *Philologica : The Malone Anniversary Studies*, ed. T. A. Kirby and H. B. Woolf, 1949, pp. 79-88.

thumbrian texts and in all texts of the transition period.[1]

(b) *h* + vowel : *eortan* 477, *elpe* 650. As in the case of the fall of *h* before a liquid this is frequently found in other late Old English texts, but traces of it are found in such an early text as the *Epinal Glossary*.[2]

(ii) The writing of *h* for *g* is represented by only two examples : *tōhēanes* 124, 421.[3]

(iii) Interchange of *ð*/*þ* and *d* :

(a) *ð*/*þ* written for *d* : *siǒne* 103, *wrixleð* 294, *lǣdaþ* (for *lǣded* 491). There are also examples where a *ð* has been corrected to *d* in the manuscript : *side* 156, *geascad* 393.

(b) *d* written for *ð*/*þ* : *singad* 635, *onwæcned* 648. This confusion of *ð*/*þ* and *d* is commonly found in the other poetic codices and other late Old English texts.[4]

(iv) Fall of a medial consonant in a group of three : *wæsmas* 243, *ferð* 415 (cf. *ferþþe* 504), *strenðu* 625. Examples are frequent in the Exeter Book and the other poetic codices.[5]

(v) Loss of final dental after a liquid or spirant : *swētes* (for *swētest* 199), a form which is kept by the latest editors. Cf. *of* (for *oft*, *Juliana* 468) and *worl* (for *world*, *Panther* 4) ; and in the other codices note *geornus* (for *geornust*, Psalm 108/16) and *lēofes* (for *lēofest*, *The Judgement Day II* 244).[6]

(vi) Nasals in unstressed syllables :

(a) *m* written for *n* : *heofumhrōfe* 173, *blīþam* 599, *mōtum* 670.[7]

---

[1] See further Schlemilch, pp. 50-1, Sievers-Brunner, 217 a. 2.

[2] Schlemilch, pp. 51-2 ; Sievers-Brunner, 217 a. 1.

[3] For an explanation of this spelling see N. Blake, 'Two Notes on the Exeter Book', *NQ*, ccvii (1962), 45-7.

[4] Schlemilch, p. 57 ; Malone, *op. cit.*

[5] Campbell, 477 ; Brook, *op. cit.*, pp. 284-5.

[6] For further examples see F. Klæber, 'Notes on OE prose texts', *MLN*, xviii (1903), 243-4.

[7] See particularly Malone, *op. cit.*

(b) Loss of final nasal : *bīgenga* 148 ; cf. *tīrfruma*,
    *inhebba* (*Crist* 206, 313). The loss of final *n*
    occurred earliest in the Northumbrian dialect
    and earlier scholars, convinced of the Northum-
    brian origin of the poem, accepted the form
    *bīgenga* as additional proof for the poem's
    Northumbrian origin. But this cannot be
    maintained, for the loss of final *n* is found in all
    the poetic codices, and although it is most
    common in Northumbrian texts, it also occurs
    in early West Saxon texts.[1]

(c) Addition of final nasal : *ēadwelan* 251 ; cf.
    *liffruman* (*Crist* 1042), etc.

## THE DEVELOPMENT OF THE PHOENIX STORY

In Egyptian sources frequent reference is made to the
*benu* (or *bennu*) bird. This bird, which plays a prominent
part in several of the Egyptian Creation-myths, was closely
associated with Heliopolis, where the temple of the sun-
god Ré (or Rá) was situated. In these myths the phoenix
usually stands as a symbol for the beginning of life and
time. But from its close connexion with the sun, which
dies and is reborn each day from the embalmed body of
the old one in the temple at Heliopolis, the bird developed as
a symbol of rebirth. Features which recur constantly in the
accounts of the benu are its cyclic return, its flight to
Heliopolis, the stand or holy tree upon which it perches,
and perfume which played an important part in the cult.
It is also often mentioned in connexion with the two
attributes of the temple at Heliopolis : the holy tree and
the fountain, also described as a spring or lake. But there
are no Egyptian sources which refer to the rebirth of the
benu by fire, its brilliant plumage or many of the other
less important details which became attached to the
phoenix myth in classical times.[2]

---

[1] P. J. Cosijn, *Altwestsächsische Grammatik*, 1888, I, pp. 188-9.

[2] On the development of the phoenix legend see Fitzpatrick,
pp. 16 ff. ; on the benu in Egypt see R. T. Rundle Clark, 'The

In his accounts of Egyptian myths and customs Herodotus describes the phoenix,[1] as he calls the bird, and it is usually thought that he referred to the Egyptian benu in his description. It is certainly from Greek that the word 'phoenix', the etymology of which is somewhat obscure, passed into other European languages. The account in Herodotus is the first detailed description of the phoenix and in it we learn that every five hundred years the phoenix returns to Heliopolis on the death of its parent. Its plumage is part red, part gold, and in shape and size it resembles the eagle—a parallel which is echoed by many later writers including the Old English poet. The phoenix carries its dead parent encased in a ball of myrrh to Heliopolis and there buries him. Herodotus does not tell us where the phoenix had its home, but in later classical authors its home is usually stated to be situated in Arabia, though sometimes in India. Among the most prominent characteristics of the phoenix in classical descriptions is its song, which is performed when it is on the point of death.[2] The first classical author to mention that the phoenix is accompanied by a crowd of other birds is Tacitus.[3] There is also a close connexion between perfume and the phoenix in classical authors. We have already noted that perfume was associated with the cult in Egypt and that Herodotus has that the phoenix encloses its parent in a ball of myrrh. The connexion between the phoenix and perfume may have been strengthened by the association of the phoenix with Arabia, the land of perfumes *par excellence*. This connexion takes one of two forms : either the phoenix constructs the nest in which it is to die out of aromatic woods and perfumes, or else certain perfumes, notably cinnamon,

Origin of the Phoenix', *University of Birmingham Historical Journal*, ii (1949–50), 1-29, 105-40 ; A. Wiedemann, *Religion of the Ancient Egyptians*, 1897, pp. 193-4 ; H. Bonnet, *Reallexikon der Ägyptischen Religionsgeschichte*, 1952, s.v. *Phönix* ; W. Helck and E. Otto, *Kleines Wörterbuch der Aegyptologie*, 1956, s.v. *Phönix*.

[1] Herodotus, *History* II, 73.

[2] M. Leroy, 'Le chant du Phénix', *L'Antiquité Classique*, i (1932), 213-31.

[3] *Annales* VI, 28.

are said to have been collected from the nest of the phoenix.[1]
Although in Egypt the benu bird could couch on any kind
of tree, in classical writing and art the phoenix is always
associated with the palm tree.[2]  In general, classical authors
have little to say about the immolation or rebirth of the
phoenix, which in Christian and late pagan authors became
the kernel of the myth.  But Pliny mentions that medicines
are gathered from the ashes of the phoenix,[3] and the renewal
of Rome under the Emperors is compared by Martial to
the rebirth of the phoenix through fire.[4]  Finally, classical
writers do not tell us much about the homeland of the
phoenix, although in Ovid it is described as a grove on a
hill *sub Elysio*.[5]  In later times, probably through the
influence of Christianity, the phoenix's home is described
as a kind of paradise, a land of perpetual spring and happiness.[6]  Thus from the time of Herodotus to the coming of
Christ the following elements may be said to be the most
prominent in the myth :  the bird has glorious plumage, it
is unique and returns to Heliopolis once in a large cycle of
time (500 years or more).  It is closely associated with the
palm tree and with cinnamon, and its home is said to be
situated in either Arabia or India.

Early in the Christian era the phoenix story achieved
its greatest popularity and is found in an extended form in
several places.  Although not all the works in which the
phoenix appears are specifically Christian, the major development of the story takes place within a Christian context.
There were, however, two different versions of the story, in
one of which the phoenix is immolated, whereas in the other

---

[1] Pliny, *Natural History* X, ii ;  XII, xlii ;  cf. J. Hubaux and
M. Leroy, 'Vulgo nascetur amomum', *Annuaire de l'Institut de
Philologie et d'Histoire Orientales*, ii (1934), 505-30.

[2] Cf. Ovid, *Metamorphoses* XV, 396.

[3] Pliny, *Natural History* XXIX, ix.

[4] *The epigrams* V, 7.  The bird is described as an Assyrian bird,
though it is usually accepted that Martial was referring to the
phoenix.

[5] *Amores* II, vi. 49-58.

[6] Cf. Sidonius Apollinaris, *Carmina* II, 407 ff., though the context
is not specifically Christian here.

it merely dies and its flesh putrefies.  The latter story
appeared already in St. Clement the Roman's *First Epistle
to the Corinthians*.[1]  The account he gives is as follows.
There is a unique bird in Arabia known as the phoenix,
which, after a lifespan of five hundred years, dies on a bier
of aromatic plants.  The flesh putrefies and produces a
worm which feeds on the flesh.  When the worm has grown
into a phoenix it takes the bones of its parent to Heliopolis
in Egypt, where it lays them on the altar of the sun.  This
is done in the sight of all and the priests dutifully note
the date of its occurrence.  There is no reference to immolation in Clement and he is the first to introduce the worm
into the story.  It is possible that Clement himself introduced this feature in order to make the parallel between
the phoenix's death and the death of men more alike.
Men's bodies decay and are the food of worms, but nevertheless will rise again at the Day of Judgement.  Yet this
branch of the story was short-lived and it is found only twice
elsewhere in Christian Latin writings.[2]

The main branch of the phoenix myth in Christian times
is that in which the phoenix is burnt and the new phoenix
arises from the ashes of the old one.  This is found for the
first time in Christian sources in the *Physiologus*, a collection
of animal fables with Christian morals, which was written
in the near east possibly as early as the second century after
Christ.[3]  It achieved immense popularity and was known
to and used by many of the church fathers, but particularly
by Ambrose.  Two early Greek versions are extant.  The
story is also mentioned in the second-century Greek
*Apocalypse of the pseudo-Baruch*, ch. 6-8.  And slightly later

---

[1] Ch. xxv-xxvi (*Pat. Gr.* I, col. 261-6).

[2] St. Cyril of Jerusalem, *Catechesis* XVIII, viii (*Pat. Gr.* XXXIII,
col. 1025-8), St. Epiphanius, *Ancoratus* LXXXIV (*Pat. Gr.* XLIII,
col. 173-4).

[3] For the development of the *Physiologus*, see F. Lauchert,
*Geschichte des Physiologus*, 1889.  M. R. James, *The Bestiary*, 1928,
pp. 2-3, however, claims that the *Physiologus* can be traced back
only as far as the fifth century and that it is unlikely to have been
written much before then.  See further F. McCulloch, *Medieval
Latin and French Bestiaries*, 2nd ed., 1962, pp. 17-19.

than this it appears in two Latin poems which are concerned entirely with the phoenix : the *Carmen de ave phoenice* attributed to Lactantius and the *Phoenix* by Claudian.[1] But these five major early Christian texts do not all have a similar account about the phoenix. The two Latin poems and one of the Greek versions of the *Physiologus* have a story which is identical in most particulars and which later became the most widespread in Europe. This account states that the phoenix is a bird which lives for a long time and then at its appointed hour it flies to Heliopolis where it dies, is reborn, and begins a new life. The characteristic elements of this version are the construction of a nest of perfume and aromatic woods, the spontaneous combustion of the nest after the phoenix's death, and the phoenix's song, which is often a type of funeral song. Death and resurrection are the most important features of this version. The other version of the myth has that the phoenix is a bird which follows the sun round on its daily course ; it does not die and there is no question of a rebirth. But having followed the sun all day, the bird is exhausted and polluted by contact with humans by the time evening comes. So each night it is revitalised and refreshed.

The poet of *The Phoenix* borrowed directly from Lactantius, and although his poem contains more than the Lactantian poem, as we shall see in a following section, the additions are not so much concerned with the phoenix as with the Christian interpretation of the symbol. It seems, therefore, unnecessary to trace the development of the phoenix story further. It must be pointed out, however, that the story was known to and frequently used by Christian writers as a symbol of the resurrection of mankind at the Day of Judgement. There are many references to

[1] All these texts have been edited together with a French translation by J. Hubaux and M. Leroy, *Le mythe du Phénix dans les littératures greque et latine*, 1939, pp. xi ff. For the *Carmen* see also Appendix I (a). English translations of the *Carmen* are available in Cook, Fitzpatrick and J. W. and A. M. Duff, *Minor Latin Poets*, 2nd ed., 1954.

the phoenix in the fathers and it is clear that the story was popular among Christians.

## PARADISE

The word *paradise* has an interesting history. It is apparently derived from a Persian word *pairidaeza*, which originally meant 'a wall, enclosure', but gradually developed the meaning of 'what was enclosed, a park, etc.'[1] It was particularly used of royal parks and pleasure grounds. The word was borrowed by the Greeks to describe the Persian walled gardens and by the Hebrews to describe any garden. The word was then used by the writers of the Septuagint for the Garden of Eden, where the idea of a physical garden is still uppermost. Finally it was used by the writers of the New Testament and later Christian writers to indicate the heavenly paradise, the abode of the blessed. The garden became symbolical. But the concept 'paradise' has not always been linked to the word *paradise*, and we must now glance at the development of the concept.

Generally the Greeks believed only in a vague shadow life for the disembodied spirit, although there are passages in Greek literature where an Elysium is described. Thus already in Homer we learn that Menelaus is to go to an Elysium, which is described in much the same terms as those used in *The Phoenix* : 'but to the Elysian plain and the bounds of the earth will the immortals convey thee . . . where life is easiest for men. No snow is there, nor heavy storm, nor ever rain, but ever does Ocean send up blasts of the shrill-blowing West Wind that they may give cooling to men.'[2] This paradise, as is true of Hesiod's Isles of the Blest,[3] was situated far out in the Western ocean on the outskirts of the world and it was reserved for ordinary men and women who had been specially favoured by the gods.

---

[1] For a similar semantic development cf. Gmc. *tūn-*, see OED, s.v. *town*.

[2] *Homer, The Odyssey*, ed. A. T. Murray, vol. I, 1953, IV, 563 ff.

[3] *Works and Days*, ll. 167 ff.

There they passed an idyllic existence. It was not long, however, before this paradise developed into an Elysium for all good and worthy men, who won it as a reward for their virtuous life on earth.[1] At the same time accounts of Utopias to be found on the world's confines, such as Plato's Atlantis, became plentiful, and it is a mark of their popularity that they were satirised by Lucian in his *True Stories*.[2] In the paradise he describes nobody grows old, it is always spring, the country abounds in fruits and flowers, and there is neither day nor night, but a perpetual half-light. The island is peaceful and there is nothing violent there. The atmosphere is pure and the air is perfumed with the scent of flowers. Music is provided by the birds and the gentle rustling of the leaves in the wind. Descriptions of this sort are not met with so frequently in the Latin writers, though Horace and Ovid both mention a terrestrial Elysium.[3] It is in the latter description that the phoenix is linked for the first time with a paradise, which in this case is the home of the pious birds. This paradise also contains a grove and the grass there is for ever green.

The coming of Christianity altered profoundly the conception and the description of the earthly paradise. The Biblical descriptions, the most important of which is found in the second chapter of Genesis, represent an Oriental tradition,[4] in which the recurring features are a high mountain in the East, a fruitful garden, a grove of trees and a river or rivers. The absence of what is harmful is implied, though not often stated. In John's vision of the new Jerusalem in Revelation, however, we find that everything harmful is excluded : 'And there shall be no more death, neither sorrow, nor crying, neither shall there be any more pain' (xxi. 4).

Christian descriptions of paradise received a strong impetus from the many apocalyptic writings which flourished

[1] See E. Rohde, *Psyche* (English Translation, 1925), and H. R. Patch, *The Other World*, 1950, pp. 16-26.
[2] *Lucian*, ed. A. M. Harmon, 1913, I, pp. 308 ff.
[3] Horace, *Epodes* XVI, 41 ff. ; Ovid, *Amores* II, vi. 49-54.
[4] Patch, *op. cit.*, pp. 7 ff.

in the early centuries of Christianity.[1] *The Apocalypse of Peter*, for example, describes paradise with its brightness, its unfading blossoms and its incorruptible plants and spices. There are no seasons and no days ; and everything is owned communally. Although these apocalyptic works were not adopted in the Biblical canon, they were very popular throughout Christendom. On the other hand, the fathers, whose main interest was in the allegorical interpretation of the earthly paradise, also included actual descriptions of paradise in their writings and these passages assured a permanent place for paradise in Christian literature. But because they so often emphasised what was not to be found there, the negative side of paradise began to predominate. The details in these descriptions remain fairly constant. Generally paradise is situated in the East, and there is perpetual spring and daylight. Trees are plentiful and the fruit on them never fails ; flowers are also often mentioned. There is a river which splits up into four streams. Some authorities even mention that there are gems which take on a special lustre in paradise. Characteristic of paradise is the absence of anything that is harmful and it is characteristic for the descriptions to be drawn up in negative terms, as in *The Phoenix*. Finally we are told that paradise is situated on a mountain which is far higher than any other mountain in this world.[2]

In this section so far I have tried to draw attention to the two separate traditions, the pagan and the Christian, of the earthly paradise. They had much in common and, in fact, they tended to be confused. This tendency was accelerated by the Christian habit of allegorising pagan authors. It is clear that the Fortunate Isles and paradise were confused by the time of Isidore, for he takes great pains to distinguish between the two.[3] Because of the

[1] For an account and texts of these apocryphal writings see M. R. James, *The Apocryphal New Testament*, 1924, and E. Hennecke, *Neutestamentliche Apokryphen*, Third edition in progress (Second ed. 1923–4).

[2] For further details see Patch, *op. cit.*, pp. 134 ff.

[3] *Etymologiarum* XIV, vi. 8 (*Pat. Lat.* LXXXII, col. 514).

similarity of the two traditions and because we know so little of the authorship of the *Carmen*, it is impossible to tell how far it is indebted to either tradition. But of even greater importance than the linking of the pagan and Christian traditions of paradise is the association of the phoenix with this paradise, which we get carried through in detail for the first time in the *Carmen*. How did this come about? It is impossible to tell, but there is clearly much that is similar in the two myths. The phoenix was associated with Arabia, the land of spices, or with India, a remote land in the East. Its habitation was far removed from man. Cinnamon, the spice most closely connected with the phoenix, is said to have been gathered in remote exotic places, which are often connected with a god.[1] It is intimately connected with springs and fountains and with trees, particularly the palm tree. The allegorical inter-pretations of the phoenix, which are found very early, con-nected the phoenix with the Deity, who in his turn is intimately connected with paradise. By Ovid's time the phoenix is connected with an Elysium, and by the time of Claudian the bird is living in a remote leafy wood. It may be that all or some of these factors contributed to the association of the phoenix with paradise. But of great interest is the account of the phoenix in Sidonius' work.[2] There the phoenix is described as living near a place not far from India where there is perpetual spring. There is no cold or frost and there are many flowers there. When the phoenix is about to die it seeks its cinnamon from this wonderful place, for its next life is dependent upon this scent. Sidonius' account is far more classical than that found in Lactantius, with which it has little in common. And although it is probable that the poem by Sidonius was written later than the *Carmen*, it might be that the phoenix came to be linked with paradise through cinnamon. The scent cinnamon was often to be found in a *locus amoenus*, which might in its turn have come to be con-sidered as the home of the phoenix as well.

[1] Herodotus, *History* III, 111 ; Pliny, *Natural History* XII, xlii.
[2] *Carmina* II, 407 ff.

## SOURCES, AUTHORSHIP AND DATE

*The Phoenix* is commonly divided into two parts (1-380, 381-677), the first of which relates the story of the phoenix and the second supplies the allegorical interpretation. Although it is dangerous to emphasise this division in *The Phoenix*, it is helpful to bear it in mind when considering the sources of the poem. The *Carmen de ave phoenice* attributed to Lactantius is the source of the first half of the poem. Unfortunately scholars have not yet come to any agreement as to whether Lactantius was in fact the author of the *Carmen* or not, and if he was whether he wrote the poem before or after his conversion to Christianity.[1] It is impossible, and indeed unnecessary, to go into the details of this dispute here ; but it must be noted that the majority of scholars now accept that Lactantius was the author. The principal argument in support of the Lactantian authorship is the testimony of the manuscripts and of several medieval writers. The earliest manuscript, Paris : Bibl. Nat. Lat. 13048, from the eighth century, makes no mention of the author, though the poem is found among others written by Venantius Fortunatus.[2] But the three next oldest manuscripts all mention that the *Carmen* was the work of Lactantius.[3] This ascription in the manuscripts is supported by some early medieval writers, among whom is Gregory of Tours. In his *De cursu stellarum*, written before 582, Gregory describes the wonders of the world, the third of which is *quod de Phinice Lactantius refert*.[4] Gregory's synopsis of the poem does not correspond in all details with the *Carmen*, but it is possible either that he was quoting from memory or that the order of the verses has become

---

[1] See especially Fitzpatrick, pp. 31 ff.

[2] For a description of the manuscript see E. A. Lowe, *Codices Latini Antiquiores*, V, 1950, p. 37.

[3] They are described by E. Baehrens, *Poetae Latini Minores*, III, 1881, pp. 247-8.

[4] Ch. xii. *Monumenta Germaniae Historica, Scriptores Rerum Merovingicarum*, tom. i, pars. 2, 1885, p. 861.

transposed.[1]  The poem is also ascribed to Lactantius in a
rhetorical work, *De dubiis nominibus*, which is found in a
ninth-century manuscript, but which was probably written
much earlier.[2]  Although a definite conclusion is not possible, it can be accepted as a working hypothesis that
Lactantius was the composer of the *Carmen*.  Lactantius
was born of heathen parents in Africa in the latter half of
the third century.  He developed a fluent Latin style, and
about 290 he was invited by Diocletian to teach rhetoric in
Bithynia.  He did not prosper there and it may have been
at this critical stage in his life that he became a Christian.
He was invited to Gaul by Constantine to tutor his son
and he died there about A.D. 340.[3]

Although Lactantius may well have been the author of
the *Carmen*, it does not follow that he wrote it after his
conversion.  Several probable Christian passages have been
pointed out in the poem, though not all scholars are pre-
pared to accept that they are in fact Christian.  At most it
can be said that Christianity is implicit in the poem.  Yet
this does not mean, as Emerson has claimed,[4] that the
English poet was the first to christianise the poem or that
he showed a great deal of originality in doing so.  Even if
Lactantius was not a Christian when he wrote the poem,
the *Carmen* was almost certainly introduced into the
Christian tradition about the phoenix shortly after its
composition, and Christian writers interpreted the poem
in a Christian way long before *The Phoenix* was written.
Gregory of Tours in his *De cursu stellarum*, ch. xii, gives a
synopsis of the poem, after which he adds : 'quod miraculum
resurrectionem humanam valde figurat et ostendit, qualiter
homo luteus redactus in pulvere, sit iterum de ipsis favillis
tuba canente resuscitandus'.  Gregory in fact attaches the
common Christian allegorical interpretation that the phoenix

---

[1] M. Leroy, 'Le chant du Phénix', *L'Antiquité Classique*, i (1932),
213-31.

[2] *Grammatici Latini*, ed. H. Keil, vol. 5, 1868, pp. 577-93.

[3] For a bibliography on Lactantius together with a short account
of his life and works, see B. Altaner, *Patrology* (translated by H. C.
Graef), 1960, pp. 208-12.  See also Fitzpatrick, pp. 31 ff.

[4] Emerson, p. 31.

represents the resurrection of man, an interpretation which was common enough in the fathers.[1] It is not necessary to believe that Gregory was the first to read the *Carmen* in this way. That the poem formed part of the Christian literature on the phoenix and paradise is confirmed by the fact that later Christian poets drew on it for their own poems. Thus in a metrical version of St. Audoenus' *Life of St. Eligius* which is extant in a ninth-century manuscript we find that the poet has drawn extensively on the *Carmen's* description of paradise.[2]

It has been suggested by G. Grau[3] that there are signs that in *The Phoenix* the poet made use of two principal sources which he was not able to harmonise completely. He suggested that apart from the *Carmen* the poet used as his other principal source a Latin poem which is variously known as *De judicio Domini, Carmen de resurrectione mortuorum* or *De die judicii*.[4] Although Grau admitted that the poet follows the sense rather than the actual words of the Latin, he nevertheless asserted that it was in this Latin poem that he found a connexion between the rebirth of the phoenix and the resurrection of Christ which served as a starting-point for his own allegory. Yet in the first half of *The Phoenix*, even though he felt himself free to alter and add to the poem, the poet follows the *Carmen* so closely that it is impossible to believe that he was using now one, now another source, particularly as the *Carmen* is so different from the *De die judicii*. Grau's arguments are very tenuous, for he failed to investigate the relationship between the various texts of the *De die judicii* and drew on now one, now another of the manuscripts for his parallels. He overlooked that the dominion of the phoenix over the other birds, which he claimed the English poet

[1] For a list of these see Fitzpatrick, pp. 12-15.

[2] N. Blake, 'Originality in "The Phoenix"', *NQ*, ccvi (1961), 326-7.

[3] G. Grau, 'Quellen und Verwandtschaften der älteren germanischen Darstellungen des Jüngsten Gerichtes', *Stud.*, xxxi (1908), 99-131.

[4] *Pat. Lat.* II, col. 1147 ff.; IV, col. 1053 ff.; LXXXIX, col. 297 ff.; and cf. Grau, *op. cit.*, pp. 35 ff.

took from the *De die judicii*, is found in other sources which he could have used. Moreover, the phoenix is mentioned only in passing in the Latin poem and the rest of it has nothing to do with the phoenix. Finally, it was common to interpret the phoenix story allegorically and we have just seen that the *Carmen* was so interpreted long before *The Phoenix* was composed. Grau's arguments carry no weight and his theory may be rejected.

The second half of the poem adds the allegorical interpretation. The phoenix story was commonly interpreted by the fathers as symbolising the resurrection of man, and there are thus many sources which the poet of *The Phoenix* could have drawn upon. But most of the references in the fathers are brief and it is generally impossible to prove that the English poet knew them, even though the possibility remains. But Gaebler has pointed out that he almost certainly used Ambrose's *Hexameron*, for there are many striking parallels between Bk. V, ch. 79-80, in which Ambrose explains the significance of the phoenix, and *The Phoenix*, lines 443 ff.[1] The passage in *The Phoenix* opens with a comparison of Christ with the palm on which the phoenix builds its nest ; whereas the Ambrose passage likens Christ to the nest (*theca*) itself. In both works this introductory passage is followed by the statement that the pious find their protection in Christ, who will come to their aid on the Day of Judgement. The allegory is then developed in *The Phoenix* by the poet's statement that a Christian builds himself a nest in that tree by reason of his good works ; a similar injunction is found in Ambrose. Each then states what these good deeds are. But in the Latin they are merely enumerated as *castitas, misericordia* and *justitia*, whereas the Old English poet expatiates on each virtue and does not follow the same order found in the Latin. But this is not surprising, for in the first half the poet treats his source freely from time to time, and it is only to be assumed that he approached his other sources in the same way. Ambrose's conclusion that anyone who

[1] H. Gaebler, 'Ueber die Autorschaft des angelsaechsischen Gedichtes vom Phoenix', *Anglia*, iii (1880), 516 ff.

is armed with these good deeds need not fear death is echoed in *The Phoenix*, where it is stated that those who have built a nest in heaven with their good deeds need not fear death. Although not all details are identical in the two accounts, they agree so closely that one must agree with Gaebler that the *Hexameron* was one of the Old English poet's sources.

In order to support his allegorical interpretation of the phoenix story, the poet includes a metrical paraphrase (lines 552 ff.) of a passage in Job in which the resurrection of man is compared to the rebirth of the phoenix. The metrical paraphrase is based on Job xxix, 18, and possibly also on Job xix, 25-6. Yet in the Vulgate there is no indication that the phoenix was mentioned by Job, as xxix, 18 reads : *In nidulo meo moriar, et sicut palma multiplicabo dies.*[1] The Septuagint here, however, uses the word *phoinix*, which in the context means 'palm', but can of course also mean 'phoenix', the Greek word being the same for both. Generally, medieval Latin writers knew only of the reading 'palm' in the verse from Job. Yet in one commentary on Job, attributed by Bede to Philip the Presbyter,[2] this confusion in the Greek which has the same word for 'palm' and 'phoenix' is noted.[3] Since this is the only Latin source which is known to link this verse in Job with the phoenix, it is possible that the commentary was known to the author of *The Phoenix*. But as it is possible that the phoenix was associated with Job in other Latin texts no longer extant and as it cannot be shown that the poet used anything else from this commentary, it can hardly be described as a source of the Old English poem.

Carleton Brown has suggested that lines 508-45 of *The Phoenix* were suggested to the poet by a passage in a work known as *De trinitate* or *In symbolum apostolorum*, formerly

---

[1] The Authorised Version has : 'I shall die in my nest, and I shall multiply my days as the sand'. The Hebrew word *khol* can mean either 'sand' or 'phoenix'.

[2] *The Complete Works of Venerable Bede*, ed. J. A. Giles, vol. 6, 1843, p. 148.

[3] Gaebler, *op. cit.*, pp. 520-21.

attributed to Ambrose.[1]  This assertion was made on the
grounds that in *The Phoenix* the judgement itself (512-17)
is said to come before the purgatorial fire, which is said to
be an echo of the passage in the *De trinitate*.[2]  In the Latin
this statement is closely linked with the phoenix story.  In
neither passage, however, is there a convincing division
between fire and judgement, and Carleton Brown has
drawn a sharp division between them which is not in fact
to be found.  The two were simultaneous : it was a judgement by fire.  And this conception is found commonly in
the fathers, for like gold man is tested by fire.[3]  But as this
theme occurs frequently in Christian writings it cannot be
proved that the poet of *The Phoenix* used the *De trinitate*
as his source here.  It is one of those many references in the
fathers which could have been used by the author of *The
Phoenix*, but which it is impossible to prove were in fact
used by him.  The only certain source of the second half of
the poem is Ambrose's *Hexameron*.

There is no indication in the Exeter Book as to who the
author of *The Phoenix* was.  Yet in the past many scholars
have suggested that the poem was composed by Cynewulf.
It was not, however, till Gaebler [4] published his article on
the authorship of the poem that this assertion was put on
a scholarly basis.  He made a minute examination of the
style of the poem, which he compared with the style of the
signed poems of Cynewulf, *Juliana*, *Crist II*, *Elene* and
*Fates*, and he came to the conclusion that Cynewulf was the
author of *The Phoenix*.  Since his time many other studies
have been carried out on the style, vocabulary, metre and
syntax of the poem in an effort to establish who the author
was.[5]  Some of the authors have claimed that their results
prove Cynewulfian authorship, but others that their work

---

[1] 'Cynewulf and Alcuin', *PMLA*, xviii (1903), 331-3.
[2] *Pat. Lat.* XVII, col. 575.
[3] A statement usually based on 1 Corinthians iii. 13-15.
[4] *Op. cit.*, pp. 488-526.
[5] C. Schaar's *Critical Studies in the Cynewulf Group*, 1949, pp. 111-
112, includes a summary of many of these earlier views ; cf. Schlotterose, pp. 88 f.

disproves it. Even the theology of *The Phoenix* has been compared with that of the signed poems.[1] Nowadays a more conservative approach to the works of Cynewulf prevails and only those poems which have a runic signature are accepted as his.[2] It is agreed that the earlier critics paid too little attention to the possibility of imitation between one poet and another and to the fact that there are many similarities between all Old English poems because of their formulaic character. Modern studies have all rejected Cynewulfian authorship of *The Phoenix*.[3] A recent investigation by O. Hietsch into the nominal compounds in *The Phoenix* comes to the same conclusion, while claiming that 'there is a considerable amount of evidence in favour of the assumption that the *Phoenix* poet was influenced both by Cynewulf's works and, to a much greater degree, especially in his paraphrase of Lactantius, by the poem of *Andreas*'.[4] We can accept, therefore, that Cynewulf is not the author of *The Phoenix*, who thus remains anonymous.

The date of the poem cannot be decided with any certainty. A *terminus ad quem* is provided by the manuscript, which is dated to *c.* 970–90. But as Sisam has shown that the anthology was probably assembled in the time of Alfred, Edward or Athelstan, the *terminus ad quem* can be taken as *c.* 940.[5] No satisfactory *terminus a quo* can be established. The accepted sources of the poem are both so early that they are of no use in dating it. Earlier authors who accepted the Cynewulfian authorship were inclined to suggest that the poem was written in the second half of the eighth century.[6] But not only is the poem not

---

[1] S. K. Das, *Cynewulf and the Cynewulf Canon*, 1942, pp. 231-2.

[2] Cynewulf and his works are investigated by K. Sisam, 'Cynewulf and his Poetry', *Studies in the History of Old English Literature*, 1953, pp. 1-28.

[3] Thus, C. Schaar, *op. cit.*, p. 326, declares that *The Phoenix* is 'clearly distinguished from the signed poems' and 'cannot be the work of Cynewulf'.

[4] O. Hietsch, 'On the Authorship of the Old English Phoenix', *Anglo-Americana*, ed. K. Brunner, 1955, p. 79.

[5] For the date of the Exeter Book, see *supra* 'The Manuscript'.

[6] So Cook, pp. xxvii-xxviii, followed by Krapp-Dobbie, p. xxxvi.

by Cynewulf, but also Cynewulf probably lived later than the eighth century. Sisam assigns him, 'whether Mercian or Northumbrian, to the ninth century'.[1] This is important, for although Cynewulf was not the author of *The Phoenix*, there are many similarities between it and his signed works which suggest that the poet lived about the same time as or slightly later than Cynewulf. So it seems likely that *The Phoenix* was written in the ninth century, possibly in the later rather than the earlier part of that century. A closer dating than this is impossible, but this date agrees well with what we know about Old English poetry. *The Phoenix* is certainly very different from poems like *Beowulf*, *Genesis* and *Daniel*, which are among the earliest poems. It has, however, much in common with the signed poems of Cynewulf and with *Andreas*, though it is possibly somewhat later than these. It is again different from the tenth-century Old English poems. It is impossible to suggest where the poem was composed, for its author is unknown, its date can be determined only within wide limits and it is impossible to decide in what dialect it was originally written. Previous commentators have suggested that it was written in Northumbria or Mercia, but they were largely influenced by the attribution of the poem to Cynewulf. We must accept, therefore, that the area in which the poem was composed cannot be decided from the evidence at our disposal.

## THE FORM

Though the poet of *The Phoenix* was following a Christian tradition in reading the *Carmen* allegorically, and an Old English tradition in translating and adapting a Latin original, we should not belittle his achievement, for not only has he had to combine and adapt different sources in order to present his allegory, but also these sources vary considerably in both content and intention. It is a tribute to the poet that he has been able to construct a homo-

[1] *Op. cit.*, p. 7.

geneous poem out of this diverse material. We must now consider how he has managed to accomplish this, and first we must see how the poet treated the *Carmen*, his principal source.

The first 380 lines of *The Phoenix* correspond to the *Carmen's* 170 lines.[1] But the English poet was by no means a slavish imitator and he adapted the original to suit his own ends. He omits, adds to or develops many of the details found in his Latin source. A typical example of how he went to work can be found in the opening lines of the poem. The *Carmen* opens : *Est locus in primo felix oriente remotus*, and this line corresponds to the opening six lines of *The Phoenix* :

> Hæbbe ic gefrugnen þætte is feor heonan
> ēastdǣlum on æþelast londa
> fīrum gefrǣge. Nis se foldan scēat
> ofer middangeard mongum gefēre
> folcāgendra, ac hē āfyrred is
> þurh Meotudes meaht mānfremmendum.

*The Phoenix* is verbose, and one might almost say diffuse, whereas the *Carmen* is precise and compact. The Latin poem states briefly that a blessed spot is to be found in the far east. But the English poet is not content with this unassumingness: he opens his poem with a flourish. He uses the typical epic formula of Old English poetry : *Hæbbe ic gefrugnen*. Similar openings are found in *Andreas* and *Beowulf*, and we can tell immediately that the poem is firmly placed in the Old English poetic tradition. The next two lines of *The Phoenix* relate what the first line of the *Carmen* has, but with some significant differences. The Latin *felix locus* appears as *æþelast londa*,

---

[1] Emerson, p. 19, has noted that of the first 380 lines in the English poem, only 148 can be said to follow the Latin. But this total is hardly a fair indication of the use of the *Carmen* in *The Phoenix*, as Emerson does not include in it phrases which are parallel to or expansions of those expressions which do translate something from the Latin. Furthermore, it is often possible that the Latin suggested something to the Old English poet, even though he did not translate the Latin literally. Emerson claimed that approximately 63 lines of the *Carmen* were not used by the English poet.

and this land is further described as being *fīrum gefrǣge*.
There is a constant attempt by the English poet to make his
landscape noble and impressive, and the word *æpele* is used
four times in the first fifty lines to describe the paradise where
the phoenix lives. He is not so much interested in the land's
beauty as in its attributes. It is not merely beautiful; it has
a deeper, more significant meaning ; and the English poet's
descriptions are always affected by the allegorical implications. The home of the phoenix is *æpele*, *wlitig* and *ǣnlīc*,
though none of these attributes is mentioned in the Latin.
In this way the poet paves the way for the allegorical interpretation which is to follow. What is implicit in the first
half is made explicit in the second. The second half is thus
the logical continuation of the first.

Yet the English poet does not leave his translation of
the first line at that, for the *remotus* has suggested something further to him. Because the land is far away, it is
not accessible to man. The poet expresses this idea within
the framework of the *nis* (*ne*) . . . *ac* construction, one of
the most characteristic rhetorical devices used in the poem.
The poet first states a negative and then its opposite :
paradise is not accessible to any man, but it is barred to all
sinners. The frequency of this construction is one of the
principal reasons for the poem's verbosity, for it is fatally
easy to multiply the negatives in the first half of the construction. Thus, in a second example of this construction a
few lines later, the *Carmen's* statement that the land was
not visited by summer's heat or winter's cold is extended
by the English poet to include among other things rain,
snow, frost, fire and hail. Consequently, although the poet
is able to achieve a fine effect as of incantation, the length
of the first clause destroys the balance of the construction
as a whole. The last clause too often comes as an anti-
climax. It is partly for this reason that we get the im-
pression from the poem that paradise is described in
negative rather than positive terms.

But to return to our consideration of the opening lines
of the poem, a further difference between *The Phoenix* and
its source should be noted. In *The Phoenix* we learn that

it is God who has ordained that this land should be far removed from sinners. God dominates the poem which is firmly and unashamedly Christian. In the *Carmen*, however, there are references only to heathen gods and goddesses, and these are included for rhetorical purposes alone. There is no suggestion in the *Carmen* that there is one deity who guides and governs all. In *The Phoenix*, on the other hand, this wonderful land is under God's strict surveillance and care (cf. 43-6).

It is not, of course, possible here to compare in detail all of the first part of *The Phoenix* with the *Carmen*. But the following general principles are characteristic of the Old English poet's approach to the *Carmen*. He made his work explicitly Christian and he tried to relate it to the Old English heroic background, as exemplified in the earlier poetry. Consequently, anything that was alien to either of these two aims was omitted. The classical gods, goddesses and heroes are all banished. Instead of Phaeton, Deucalion, Phoebus, Aurora and Aeolus we have the Christian God, who is alone said to guide and direct all things. Other classical references to such things as Olympus and the constellation Cancer are likewise omitted. The English poet has not attempted, however, to shift the scene of action from the far and the near east. The phoenix is said to visit *Syrwara lond* (166). The English poet has also rejected the *Carmen's* list of precious spices, which are gathered by the phoenix as it prepares for death. Although their names were possibly familiar to educated Englishmen who would be able to read Latin, there were no English words for many of them and the English poet no doubt felt that they were not sufficiently naturalised for inclusion in his poem. As a result, the poem has lost some of the richness and ornateness of the Latin. Nevertheless, it can hardly be doubted that it was right to exclude those terms, for they would have been out of place in the reworking of the story.

In order to fill the vacuum created by leaving out all that might be considered classical, the English poet has set his poem against a Christian Germanic background. Instead of classical gods and heroes we have a Christian

God with copious references to such events as the Day of Judgement. This event was introduced as a result of the allegorical interpretation : the fire of the phoenix symbolises the fire of judgement in which the souls are tested and the good souls purified, and the rebirth of the phoenix symbolises the resurrection of man on that fatal day. There are many other instances like this where the allegory intrudes into the first half, most of which are pointed out in the notes. In order not to misunderstand this feature it is necessary to bear in mind the nature of medieval allegory. The world to medieval man was the creation of the divine logos. Consequently every created thing was an expression of the divine thought ; the world in fact was a book written by the hand of God in which every creature is a word charged with meaning. By reading nature aright, the wise man can look beyond the material form and penetrate to the divine thought of which it is the material expression. In a word the whole world is a symbol. Consequently, for the Old English Christian poet of *The Phoenix* the bird is merely a symbol of a divine truth. The poem was written in order that we might realise what this truth was. The poet probes the meaning of the natural symbol. It must be emphasised, therefore, that for the poet the most important fact is the allegorical interpretation of the symbol. The phoenix in itself is merely one of the many natural ways in which this Christian truth finds expression, and as such is neither more nor less important than the story of the seed (242 ff.) which is a symbol for the same Christian truth. So it need not surprise us that the allegory keeps on appearing in the first half, for the symbol and the interpretation are one and the same thing. One is the divine thought and the other is the expression of that thought in a material form. We today may perhaps find the story of the phoenix more enjoyable than the allegorical interpretation. Many modern critical works stress the great beauty of the descriptions in the first half of this poem. But we must not forget that for the poet these were subservient to his real purpose, the revelation of the Christian message to be found in a created being. But as

the phoenix was only a symbol for the poet, this was bound
to affect his attitude to his source. He would take only
that which served his purpose.

It is interesting to note how the poet sets his poem
against a Germanic background. We have already seen
how he uses the Old English epic opening. There are also
many descriptive touches which are clearly influenced by
earlier descriptions. Thus the *Carmen's Atque ubi Sol
pepulit fulgentis limina portae* (43) appears in *The Phoenix* as:

> Sōna swā sēo sunne    sealte strēamas
> hēa oferhlīfað.    (120-21)

Instead of the classical gates of heaven, the sea which
appears so often in Old English poetry is introduced. And
there is in *The Phoenix* frequent reference to both sun and
sea. But one should pay particular attention to the poet's
use of words drawn from the Old English heroic vocabulary,
such as *wælrēaf, beaducræftig, heaporōf* and *ānhaga*. These
words which are reminiscent of more vigorous and blood-
thirsty exploits appear at first to be incongruous in a poem
which portrays a peaceful idyll of happiness and joy. But
they are included to make plain the correspondence between
the life of the phoenix and that of man, the symbol and the
thing symbolised. The phoenix's life, death and rebirth
stand for the life, death and future resurrection of man.
In order to make this plain the poet tends to anthro-
pomorphise the phoenix. Thus the bird is described in
terms like those above which would be more appropriate
to Old English heroes ; its nest is described as a *hūs*, a
*willsele* and a *hof* ; the bird collects its ashes and bones
'from the grave' (267) as men will do on the Day of Judgement ; and the bird emerges from the fire 'purged of sins'
(242). This last phrase reminds us of the blessed who will
come through the purgatorial fire purged of their sins.
One cannot deny that to us the result is sometimes jarring,
but in this way the poet has cleverly linked the symbol
to the thing symbolised and he has thus prevented the
poem from falling into two halves.[1]

[1] See further Blake.

*The Phoenix* differs considerably from the earlier poems in the mood created by the natural descriptions. The earlier poets portrayed nature in its sternest moods and their descriptions are both vigorous and positive. The poet of *The Phoenix*, however, portrays an imaginary, ideal landscape. Everything is pleasant, nothing is harmful. His descriptions therefore have none of the reality of those in the earlier poetry and he portrays the land in very negative terms. This does not mean that we should agree with Moorman, who claims that 'the poem marks the decadence of the descriptive powers of pre-conquest poetry'.[1] The poet is not trying to create the same effect as the earlier poets, and their descriptions are hardly comparable. In *The Phoenix* we are to imagine at one and the same time a real garden and a spiritual haven, a terrestrial and a heavenly paradise. To have concentrated too much on the material side of the garden might have lessened our appreciation of its more spiritual qualities. The essential unity of the poem would also have been endangered, as the two halves would have become two separate entities : the first the story, the second the interpretation. Therefore the descriptions tend not to be visual, and when we compare *The Phoenix* with the *Carmen* we see that the English descriptions have lost much of that precision and detail which are to be found in the Latin. An example of this is the description of the *fons* in the garden. In the *Carmen* this is described as *perspicuus, lenis, dulcibus uber aquis* (26), whereas in *The Phoenix* it is merely mentioned as *wæter wynsumu* (65). It could be said that *wynsumu* here means hardly more than 'pleasant', but yet it carries with it overtones of that unalloyed pleasure which one experiences not only in this pleasant land but also in heaven. For *wyn* as either a simplex or an element of a compound is one of the poet's favourite words, and apart from *wyn* itself we find *wynlīc, wynlond* and *wynsum*. The difficulty the poet came up against was how to express in positive terms what heaven means to the soul, a difficulty he tried to solve by a

[1] F. W. Moorman, *The Interpretation of Nature in English Poetry from Beowulf to Shakespeare*, 1905, p. 43.

heavy reliance on adjectives expressive of joy, majesty, light and bliss. These adjectives are in one sense more fitting in the allegorical interpretation than in the story of the phoenix. But this is to make a distinction between the story and its meaning, a distinction which, as we have seen, the poet did not make, for to him they were one. He naturally painted the garden in more symbolic terms than those found in his source. So *wynsumu* in line 65 also implies the pleasantness of the heavenly home. Thus in order to appreciate the poem we must look through the actual material objects to what they represent ; we can read the phoenix story in the first half only in the light of the allegorical interpretation. It has no existence in its own right.

So far we have been considering the way in which the poet of *The Phoenix* handled his principal source, the *Carmen*, in the first half of the poem. It is time now to turn to a brief consideration of his treatment of Ambrose's *Hexameron*, which he used in the second half. Not unnaturally the problems here were different, for the source was both Christian and allegorical already. The poet's task was to relate the material found in Ambrose to the story he had told earlier and to work Ambrose's allegorical interpretation into the general allegory which he was drawing in the second half. Ambrose for his part when he wrote the *Hexameron* had not been interested in presenting a complete account of the phoenix. He was able to select those details of the story which would help to illustrate the moral he was drawing. His use of the phoenix story was therefore limited. But the English poet chose to base his poem on the complete phoenix story, which is then used as the basis for the allegory. So, though the story can to some extent be altered to suit the allegory, it must in itself be logical and coherent. Not only had the poet to take the demands of his story into consideration, but he had also to relate the allegory found in Ambrose to other allegorical interpretations of that story. Ambrose provided him with only one way of reading the phoenix story. He clearly, however, knew many other ways of reading it, even though it is not certain whether he had learned of these from written or oral sources. Consequently, the interpretation in the *Hexameron* was altered somewhat to meet these requirements. Even so the poet has not managed to present a unified allegory. But in order to show this it might be best to glance briefly at the development of the allegory.

The allegory opens with the description of the expulsion of our forefathers from Eden after they had tasted the apple (393 ff.). They were forced to leave that blessed plain (418) which was then barred to them until Christ by his death here on earth reopened it. The expulsion of Adam and Eve from Eden resembles the flight of the phoenix from its home when it is old (428 ff.). But whereas the phoenix leaves to become rejuvenated and then returns home, man wanders in the world afflicted by the powers of evil. Nevertheless, some men in this world obey the commands of Christ (443 ff.). The allegory is now developed by comparing the tree in which the phoenix built its nest with Christ. If a man shelters in Christ nothing can harm him, as nothing could harm the phoenix in its nest (cf. 179-81). To shelter in Christ man must build a nest by means of his good works, which correspond to the spices used by the phoenix to construct its nest. By these good deeds a man earns admission to the heavenly home. But first at his death he is buried and waits in his grave till Doomsday (489-90). At Doomsday all are led before God in judgement and the world is consumed by fire (491 ff.). Then the sign of the phoenix, by which we are to understand God, or more likely Christ (cf. 646-7), will be revealed to men when all the dead take on a new body and come to judgement. The blessed are happy, for they have won salvation by their good works and they rise to glory having been purged by fire (518 ff.). At this point the poet includes the metrical paraphrase of Job (546 ff.). Job is certain he will rise again at the Day of Judgement, just as the phoenix rose again from its ashes. This leads to a restatement of the allegory with a slightly different emphasis ; as the phoenix is reborn, so will the souls of good men be reunited with their bodies and together they will rise to heaven (570 ff.). In heaven the blessed follow Christ around in a great company, as the birds had followed the phoenix (589 ff.). Yet, like the phoenix, the blessed live in glory and are clothed in shining garments. In heaven there is no sorrow, pain or anything harmful, just as all these hurtful things had been excluded from the home of the phoenix (611 ff., cf. 50 ff.). The blessed sing the praises of Christ in heaven. The poet then briefly introduces the story of the Resurrection and the rebirth of the phoenix is now compared with the death and resurrection of Christ (638 ff.). As the phoenix gathers spices in his wings when he is eager for rebirth, so Christ gave us eternal life by his death here on earth (642-54). The poem then concludes with praises to God.

This synopsis of the second half reveals that the poet has not confined himself to simple allegory, for the details of the story can be interpreted in several different ways. Thus the phoenix represents at first all men who will rise again at Doomsday, then more narrowly all good men who will go to heaven, and finally Christ himself. The phoenix's rebirth foreshadows man's future resurrection, but is also a symbol of Christ's past resurrection. Consequently, a certain amount of confusion can arise, for the blessed are sometimes compared with the phoenix and sometimes with the birds which follow the phoenix. Likewise Christ is represented in the original story either by the tree or by the phoenix itself. The poet has failed to select and arrange his material satisfactorily, for the overlapping interpretations sometimes confuse the reader. One should not of course expect a perfect concordance between the story and the allegory, though the method the poet has chosen of presenting first the story and then the allegory invites one to extend the allegory to the entire story. But this is impossible, for though the poet has chosen to present the entire phoenix story, he has used only individual scenes from that story to illustrate the various Christian themes which he wished to exemplify. The allegory is fragmentary and this tends to prevent a proper fusion of the two halves, as they are not satisfactorily balanced against each other. One can agree

that by refusing to confine himself to one allegory the poet
has given his work greater significance and depth ; but
nevertheless one cannot help feeling that a greater poet
would have been able to order the various allegorical
strands into an organic unity. The interweaving of the
different interpretations in *The Phoenix* has not been carried
out with sufficient subtlety. They are too isolated and too
fragmentary. The poet is never able to suggest that the
phoenix story symbolises all these Christian themes at one
and the same time. The fault may well be that the poet
knew too many different interpretations of the phoenix and
attempted to include them all without, however, being able
to combine them into a comprehensive pattern.

The failure to provide a comprehensive allegory under-
mines to some extent the poet's attempt to unify the two
halves of the poem, which consists in constantly anticipating
the allegory in the first half and by constantly looking
back to the phoenix story in the second half. Thus the
details of the phoenix story are often coloured by their
allegorical attributes. The phoenix in the first half is
described as *se tīrēadga, þēodne mǣrum, se clǣna, se mōdga,*
*þone hālgan, se gesǣliga* and *se ēadga,* all of which appella-
tions clearly look forward to the Christian interpretation,
particularly as many of them are later applied to Christ or
the blessed. We have already seen that the same applies
to *wlitig* and adjectives like it. But there are, furthermore,
many verbal parallels between the two halves which serve
to link them even more closely. Even the opening of the
phoenix story *Hæbbe ic gefrugnen* is echoed by that of the
opening of the allegory *Habbaþ wē geascad* (393). More
important echoes are such verbal parallels as

> Ne mæg him bitres wiht
> scyldum sceððan    (179-80)

> þǣr him wihte ne mæg
> ealdfēonda nān    ātre sceþþan,
> fācnes tācne    on þā frēcnan tīd.    (448-50)

And passages with the *nis (ne)* . . . *ac* construction are
found in both halves to describe paradise (cf. 611 ff.,

50 ff.).[1] Sometimes, however, the allegory intrudes too forcefully in the first half and sometimes an incomplete fusion of story and allegory leads to confusion and uncertainty.[2]

*The Phoenix* then represents a valiant attempt by a sensitive poet to produce an Old English poem out of a mixture of a late classical Latin poem and some Christian themes. The attempt is not altogether successful for the poet has not been ruthless enough in selecting and arranging his material. Though he has substantially altered the *Carmen*, he has not tailored the allegorical interpretations adequately to the measure of the story that he adapted from the *Carmen*. The poem is composed in a simple, fairly plain style, the major fault of which is a tendency to repetition. The poet repeats too many of his favourite phrases, he overworks the *nis* (*ne*) . . . *ac* construction, and he starts far too many of his sentences with *þonne*. He can, however, at times make use of striking similes and words. The poem's beauty lies in its idyllic tone, in the picture of a terrestrial-heavenly paradise, and in the gracefulness with which some of the allegorical interpretations are linked with the story of the phoenix. It has indeed a quiet charm and simple dignity which are not found elsewhere in the whole of Old English poetry.

[1] A list of the major correspondences between the two halves can be found in A. S. Cook and C. B. Tinker, *Select Translations from Old English Poetry*, 1935, p. 144.

[2] See notes to lines 6, 12, 314-17, 579-80, etc.

# SELECT BIBLIOGRAPHY

## MANUSCRIPT AND FACSIMILES

BRITISH MUSEUM Additional MS 9067. A transcript of the
Exeter Book made by R. Chambers in 1831 and collated
by Sir F. Madden in 1831–2.

CHAMBERS, R. W., FÖRSTER, M., AND FLOWER, R. *The Exeter
Book of Old English Poetry.* London, 1933.

KER, N. R. *Catalogue of Manuscripts containing Anglo-Saxon.*
Oxford, 1957.

SCHIPPER, J. 'Zum Codex Exoniensis', *Germania*, xix (1874),
327-38.

SISAM, K. 'The Exeter Book', *Studies in the History of Old
English Literature.* Oxford, 1953, pp. 97-108.

## EDITIONS OF *THE PHOENIX*

The line references in brackets indicate the extent of partial
editions.

ARDERN, P. S. *First Readings in Old English.* Second
edition. Wellington, 1951. [1-14a, 21b-27, 50-84.]

BRIGHT, J. W. *An Anglo-Saxon Reader.* New York, 1891.
(Third edition, revised. New York, 1894.)

CARPENTER, S. H. *An Introduction to the Study of the Anglo-
Saxon Language.* Boston, 1875. [1-84.]

CONYBEARE, J. J. 'Account of an Anglo-Saxon Paraphrase of
the Phoenix attributed to Lactantius', *Archæologia*, xvii
(1814), 193-7. [1-27, 81b-84.]

CONYBEARE, J. J., AND W. D. *Illustrations of Anglo-Saxon
Poetry.* London, 1826. [1-27, 81b-84.]

COOK, A. S. *The Old English Elene, Phoenix, and Physiologus.*
New Haven, 1919.

ETTMÜLLER, L. *Engla and Seaxna Scôpas and Bôceras.*
Quedlinburg and Leipzig, 1850.

GOLLANCZ, I. *The Exeter Book*, part I. EETS Original Series
104. London, 1895.

GREIN, C. W. M. *Bibliothek der angelsächsischen Poesie*, vol. I.
Göttingen, 1857.

GRUNDTVIG, N. F. S. *Phenix-Fuglen, et angelsachsisk Kvad.* Copenhagen, 1840.

KAISER, R. *Medieval English.* Third edition. Berlin, 1958. [1-59, 71-84, 667-77.]

KLAEBER, F. *The Later Genesis and other Old English and Old Saxon Texts relating to the Fall of Man.* Heidelberg, 1913. [393-423, 437b-42.]

KLIPSTEIN, L. F. *Analecta Anglo-Saxonica,* vol. II. New York and London, 1849.

KÖRNER, K. *Einleitung in das Studium des Angelsächsischen,* 2. Teil. Heilbronn, 1880. [1-84.]

KRAPP, G. P., AND DOBBIE, E. v. K. *The Exeter Book.* The Anglo-Saxon Poetic Records, vol. III. New York, 1936.

ROBINSON, W. C. *Introduction to our Early English Literature.* London, 1885. [1-84.]

SCHLOTTEROSE, O. 'Die altenglische Dichtung "Phoenix" ', *BBA,* xxv (1908).

SWEET, H. *An Anglo-Saxon Reader.* Oxford, 1876. (Ninth edition revised by C. T. Onions, 1922.) [1-84.]

THORPE, B. *Codex Exoniensis.* Published for the Society of Antiquaries. London, 1842.

WANLEY, H. *Antiquæ Literaturæ Septentrionalis Liber Alter,* etc. (Vol. II of Hickes, G., *Linguarum Vett. Septentrionalium Thesaurus.*) Oxford, 1705. [1-2, 667-77.]

WRIGHT, T. *St. Patrick's Purgatory.* London, 1844. [1-84.]

WÜLCKER, R. P. *Bibliothek der angelsächsischen Poesie,* vol. III. Leipzig, 1898.

WYATT, A. J. *An Anglo-Saxon Reader.* Cambridge, 1919. [1-59.]

ZUPITZA, J., AND SCHIPPER, J. *Alt- und mittelenglisches Übungsbuch.* Vienna and Leipzig, 1897. [1-27, 78-89, 182-264, 320-80, 583-677.]

## TRANSLATIONS OF *THE PHOENIX*

Unless otherwise stated translations are in English. The line references in brackets indicate the extent of partial translations.

BROWN, A. R. 'The Happy Land. Cynewulf's Phoenix', *Poet-lore,* II (1890), 523-5. [1-84.]

CONYBEARE, J. J., AND W. D. *Illustrations of Anglo-Saxon Poetry.* London, 1826. (Also *Archæologia,* xvii (1814),

193-7.)  [1-27, English and Latin ;  81b-84, Latin.]

COOK, A. S., AND TINKER, C. B.  *Select Translations from Old English Poetry*.  Revised edition.  Harvard, 1935.

FAUST, C., AND THOMSON, S.  *Old English Poems, Translated into the Original Meter*.  Chicago, 1918.

GOLLANCZ, I.  *The Exeter Book*, part I.  EETS Original Series 104.  London, 1895.

GORDON, R. K.  *Anglo-Saxon Poetry*.  Revised edition.  London, 1954.

GREIN, C. W. M.  *Der Vogel Phönix, ein angelsächsisches Gedicht, stabreimend übersetzt*.  Rinteln, 1854.  [German.]

GREIN, C. W. M.  *Dichtungen der Angelsachsen stabreimend übersetzt*, vol. I.  Göttingen, 1857.  [German.]

GRUNDTVIG, N. F. S.  *Phenix-Fuglen, et angelsachsisk Kvad*.  Copenhagen, 1840.  [Danish.]

HALL, J. L.  *Judith, Phoenix, and other Anglo-Saxon Poems*.  New York, 1902.

HAMMERICH, F.  *De episk-kristelige Oldkvad hos de gotiske Folk*.  Copenhagen, 1873.  [1-84, Danish.]

KENNEDY, C. W.  *The Poems of Cynewulf Translated into English Prose*.  London, 1910.

KENNEDY, C. W.  *Early English Christian Poetry Translated into Alliterative Verse*.  London, 1952.

KENNEDY, C. W.  *An Anthology of Old English Poetry Translated into Alliterative Verse*.  New York, 1960.  [1-392.]

KLIPSTEIN, L. F.  *Analecta Anglo-Saxonica*, vol. II.  New York and London, 1849.  [33-68a.]

KÖRNER, K.  *Einleitung in das Studium des Angelsächsischen*, 2. Teil.  Heilbronn, 1880.  [1-84, German.]

OLIVERO, F.  *Traduzioni dalla poesia anglo-sassone con introduzione e note*.  Bari, 1915.  [85-152, 182-219a, 240b-64, 291-319, Italian.]

ROBINSON, W. C.  *Introduction to our Early English Literature*.  London, 1895.  [1-84.]

SCHLOTTEROSE, O.  'Die altenglische Dichtung "Phoenix"', *BBA*, xxv (1908).  [German.]

SIMS, W. R.  'The Happy Land : from the Phoenix', *MLN*, vii (1892), 11-13.  [1-84.]

SPAETH, J. D.  *Old English Poetry.  Translations into Alliterative Verse with Introduction and Notes*.  Princeton, 1921.  [1-264, 570-677.]

STEPHENS, G.  'The King of Birds ; or, the Lay of the Phoenix :

an Anglo-Saxon Song of the Tenth or Eleventh Century',
*Archæologia*, xxx (1844), 256-322. (Also printed separately
London, 1844.)

THORPE, B. *Codex Exoniensis.* Published for the Society of
Antiquaries. London, 1842.

WRIGHT, T. *St. Patrick's Purgatory.* London, 1844. [1-84.]


## TEXTUAL STUDIES, ETC.

AHRENS, J. *Darstellung der Syntax im angelsächsischen Gedicht
'Phoenix'.* Diss. Rostock, 1904.

BARNOUW, A. J. *Textkritische Untersuchungen nach dem
Gebrauch des bestimmten Artikels und des schwachen
Adjektivs in der altenglischen Poesie.* Diss. Leiden, 1902.

BAUER, H. *Ueber die Sprache und Mundart der altenglischen
Dichtungen Andreas, Gûðlâc, Phönix, hl. Kreuz und
Höllenfahrt Cristi.* Marburg, 1890.

BLACKBURN, F. A. 'Note on the Phoenix, Verse 151', *MLN*,
x (1895), 259-60.

BLAKE, N. F. 'Originality in "The Phoenix" ', *NQ*, ccvi (1961),
326-7.

BLAKE, N. F. 'Two Notes on the Exeter Book', *NQ*, ccvii
(1962), 45-7.

BLAKE, N. F. 'Some problems of Interpretation and Translation in the OE *Phoenix*', *Anglia*, lxxx (1962), 50-62.

BRADSHAW, M. R. 'The Versification of the Old English Poem
Phoenix', *American Journal of Philology*, xv (1894), 454-68.

BRETT, C. 'Notes on Old and Middle English', *Modern
Language Review*, xxii (1927), 257-64.

BROWN, C. F. 'Cynewulf and Alcuin', *PMLA*, xviii (1903),
308-34.

COOK, A. S. 'Phoenix 56', *MLN*, xiv (1899), 450-1.

COSIJN, P. J. 'Anglosaxonica III', *Beitr.*, xxi (1896), 8-26.

COSIJN, P. J. 'Anglosaxonica IV', *Beitr.*, xxiii (1898), 109-30.

CREMER, M. *Metrische und sprachliche Untersuchung der
altenglischen Gedichte Andreas, Guðlac, Phoenix (Elene,
Juliana, Crist).* Diss. Bonn, 1888.

EKWALL, E. [Review of Cook's edition.] *AB*, xxxiii (1922), 61-7.

EMERSON, O. F. 'Originality in Old English Poetry', *RES*, ii
(1926), 18-31.

FULTON, E. 'On the Authorship of the Anglo-Saxon Poem
Phoenix', *MLN*, xi (1896), 146-69.

P.—D

GAEBLER, H. 'Ueber die Autorschaft des angelsaechsischen Gedichtes vom Phoenix', *Anglia*, iii (1880), 488-526.

GRAU, G. 'Quellen und Verwandtschaften der älteren germanischen Darstellungen des Jüngsten Gerichtes', *Stud.*, xxxi (1908).

HART, J. M. 'Allotria', *MLN*, xiv (1899), 316-17.

HIETSCH, O. 'On the Authorship of the Old English Phoenix', *Anglo-Americana*, presented to Dr. L. Hibler-Lebmannsport, edited by K. Brunner, Stuttgart, 1955, pp. 72-9.

HOLTBUER, F. 'Der syntaktische Gebrauch des Genetives in Andreas, Gûðlac, Phönix, dem heiligen Kreuz und Höllenfahrt', *Anglia*, viii (1885), 1-40.

HOLTHAUSEN, F. 'Zum Schluss des altengl. "Phönix"', *Archiv für das Studium der neueren Sprachen und Literaturen*, cxii (1904), 132-3.

HOLTHAUSEN, F. 'Altenglische Kleinigkeiten', *Germanisch-romanische Monatsschrift*, N.F. iii (1953), 345.

KERN, J. H. 'Phoenix 25', *Neophilologus*, xii (1927), 193.

KLAEBER, F. 'Emendations in Old English Poems', *Modern Philology*, ii (1904–5), 141-6.

KLAEBER, F. 'Phenix, 386', *JEGP*, vi (1906–7), 198.

KLAEBER, F. 'Notes on Old English Poems, No. 10', *JEGP*, xii (1913), 258.

KOCK, E. A. 'Jubilee Jaunts and Jottings', *Lunds Universitets Årsskrift*, N.F. Avd. i, Bd. XIV, Nr. 26, 1918.

PLANER, J. *Untersuchungen über die syntaktischen Gebrauch des Verbums in dem angelsächsischen Gedicht vom Phoenix.* Diss. Leipzig, 1892.

SCHAUBERT, E. VON, 'Zur Erklärung Schwierigkeiten bietender altenglischer Textstellen', *Philologica : The Malone Anniversary Studies*, edited by T. A. Kirby & H. B. Woolf, Baltimore, 1949, pp. 31-42.

SHEARIN, H. G. 'The *Phoenix* and the *Guthlac*', *MLN*, xxii (1907), 263.

TUPPER, F. (JR.) 'Textual Criticism as a Pseudo-Science', *PMLA*, xxv (1910), 164-81.

## LACTANTIUS AND THE *CARMEN DE AVE PHOENICE*

BAEHRENS, A. *Poetae Latini Minores*, vol. III. Leipzig, 1881.

DUFF, J. W., AND A. M. *Minor Latin Poems*. The Loeb

Classical Library 284. Second edition. London and Cambridge, U.S.A., 1954.

FITZPATRICK, M. C. *Lactanti de ave phoenice.* Diss. Philadelphia, 1933.

LABRIOLLE, P. de. *Histoire de la littérature latine chrétienne.* Paris, 1920.

LEROY, M. 'Le chant du Phénix. L'Ordre des vers dans le Carmen de ave Phoenice', *L'Antiquité Classique,* i (1932), 213-31.

MANITIUS, M. *Geschichte der christlich-lateinischen Poesie bis zur Mitte des 8. Jahrhunderts.* Stuttgart, 1891.

RICHMOND, O. L. *De ave phoenice.* Edinburgh, 1947.

RIESE, A. *Anthologia Latina pars prima,* vol. II. Second edition. Leipzig, 1906.

SCHUSTER, M. 'Zur Echtheitsfrage und Abfassungszeit von Lactantius' Dichtung *De ave Phoenice',* *Wiener Studien,* liv (1936), 118-28.


## GENERAL WORKS ON *THE PHOENIX*
### AND ALLIED TOPICS

HUBAUX, J., AND LEROY, M. 'Vulgo nascetur amomum', *Annuaire de l'Institut de Philologie et d'Histoire Orientales (Mélanges Bidez),* ii (1934), 505-30.

LAUCHERT, F. *Geschichte des Physiologus.* Strassburg, 1889.

LAURENT, M. 'Le phénix, les serpents et les aromates dans une miniature du XIIe siècle', *L'Antiquité Classique,* iv (1935), 375-401.

PATCH, H. R. *The Other World according to descriptions in Medieval Literature.* Cambridge, U.S.A., 1950.

ROHDE, E. *Psyche, The Cult of Souls and Belief in Immortality among the Greeks.* English translation. London, 1925.

RUNDLE CLARK, R. T. 'The Origin of the Phoenix', *University of Birmingham Historical Journal,* ii (1949-50), 1-29, 105-140.

SBORDONE, F. 'La fenice nel culto di Helios', *Rivista indo-greco-italica,* xix (1935), 1-46.

WIEDEMANN, M. 'Die Phönix-Sage im alten Aegypten', *Zeitschrift für Aegyptische Sprache und Alterthumskunde,* xvi (1878), 89-106.

## LITERARY BACKGROUND AND LANGUAGE

ABBETMEYER, C. *Old English Poetical Motives derived from the Doctrine of Sin.* Baltimore, 1903.

ANDERSON, G. K. *The Literature of the Anglo-Saxons.* Oxford, 1949.

BRUNNER, K. *Altenglische Grammatik nach der Angelsächsischen Grammatik von E. Sievers.* Second edition. Halle, 1951.

CAMPBELL, A. *Old English Grammar.* Oxford, 1959.

DAS, S. K. *Cynewulf and the Cynewulf Canon.* Calcutta, 1942.

DEERING, W. *The Anglo-Saxon Poets on the Judgment Day.* Halle, 1890.

KENNEDY, C. W. *The Earliest English Poetry.* New York and London, 1943.

KLUGE, F. 'Zu altenglischen Dichtungen. 3. Zum Phönix', *Englische Studien,* viii (1885), 474-9.

LARSEN, H. 'Notes on the Phoenix', *JEGP,* xli (1942), 79-84.

MALONE, K. 'When did Middle English begin ?' *Curme Volume of Linguistic Studies (Language Monograph,* No. 7, 1930), 110-17.

MARCKWARDT, A. H. 'Verb Inflections in Late Old English', *Philologica : The Malone Anniversary Studies,* edited by T. A. Kirby & H. B. Woolf. Baltimore, 1949, pp. 79-88.

SCHAAR, C. *Critical Studies in the Cynewulf Group.* Lund and Copenhagen, 1949.

SCHLEMILCH, W. 'Beiträge zur Sprache und Orthographie spätaltengl. Sprachdenkmäler der Übergangszeit (1000–1150)', *Stud.,* xxxiv (1914).

WARNER, R. D.-N. *Early English Homilies from the Twelfth Century MS. Vesp. D. xiv.* EETS Original Series 152. London, 1917.

# THE PHOENIX

# THE PHOENIX

Hæbbe ic gefrugnen   þætte is feor heonan
ēastdǣlum on   æþelast londa
fīrum gefrǣge.   Nis se foldan scēat
ofer middangeard   mongum gefēre

5 folcāgendra,   ac hē āfyrred is
þurh Meotudes meaht   mānfremmendum.
Wlitig is se wong eall,   wynnum geblissad
mid þām fægrestum   foldan stencum,
ænlīc is þæt īglond,   æþele se Wyrhta
10 mōdig meahtum spēdig,   sē þā moldan gesette.
Ðǣr bið oft open,   ēadgum tōgēanes
onhliden hlēoþra wyn,   heofonrīces duru.
Þæt is wynsum wong,   wealdas grēne
rūme under roderum.   Ne mæg þǣr rēn ne snāw
15 ne forstes fnǣst   ne fȳres blǣst
he hægles hryre   ne hrīmes dryre
ne sunnan hǣtu   ne sincaldu
ne wearm weder   ne winterscūr
wihte gewyrdan,   ac se wong seomað
20 ēadig ond onsund.   Is þæt æþele lond
blōstmum geblōwen.   Beorgas þǣr ne muntas
stēape ne stondað,   ne stānclifu
hēah hlīfiað,   swā hēr mid ūs,
ne dene ne dalu   ne dūnscrafu,
25 hlǣwas ne hlincas,   ne þǣr hleonað ōo
unsmēþes wiht,   ac se æþela feld
wrīdað under wolcnum   wynnum geblōwen.
Is þæt torhte lond,   twelfum hērra
folde fæðmrīmes,   swā ūs gefreogum glēawe
30 wītgan þurh wīsdōm   on gewritum cȳþað,
þonne ænig þāra beorga   þe hēr beorhte mid ūs
hēa hlīfiað   under heofontunglum.
Smylte is se sigewong : sunbearo līxeð,
wuduholt wynlīc,   wæstmas ne drēosað,
35 beorhte blēde,   ac þā bēamas ā

15. fnǣst : *MS* fnæft, n *written on an erasure.*

45

grēne stondað,   swā him God bibēad.
Wintres ond sumeres   wudu bið gelīce
blēdum gehongen.   Nǣfre brosniað
f.56b      lēaf under lyfte   ne him līg sceþeð
40   ǣfre tō ealdre,   ǣrþon edwenden
worulde geweorðe.   Swā iū wǣtres þrym
ealne middangeard,   mereflōd þeahte
eorþan ymbhwyrft,   þā se æþela wong
ǣghwǣs onsund   wið ȳðfare
45   gehealden stōd   hrēora wǣga
ēadig unwemme   þurh ēst Godes,
bīdeð swā geblōwen   oð bǣles cyme,
Dryhtnes dōmes   þonne dēaðrǣced,
hǣleþa heolstorcofan   onhliden weorþað.
50   Nis þǣr on þām londe   lāðgenīðla
ne wōp ne wracu,   wēatācen nān,
yldu ne yrmðu   ne se enga dēað
ne līfes lyre   ne lāþes cyme
ne synn ne sacu   ne sārwracu
55   ne wǣdle gewin   ne welan onsȳn
ne sorg ne slǣp   ne swār leger ;
ne wintergeweorp   ne wedra gebregd
hrēoh under heofonum   ne se hearda forst
caldum cylegicelum   cnyseð ǣnigne ;
60   þǣr ne hægl ne hrīm   hrēosað tō foldan
ne windig wolcen,   ne þǣr wǣter fealleþ
lyfte gebysgad,   ac þǣr lagustrēamas,
wundrum wrǣtlīce   wyllan onspringað
fǣgrum foldwylmum.   Foldan leccaþ
65   wǣter wynsumu   of þæs wuda midle,
þā mōnþa gehwām   of þǣre moldan tyrf
brimcald brecað,   bearo ealne geondfarað
þrāgum þrymlīce.   Is þæt Þēodnes gebod
þætte twelf sīþum   þæt tīrfæste
70   lond geondlāce   laguflōda wynn.
Sindon þā bearwas   blēdum gehongne,
wlitigum wæstmum.   Þǣr nō woniað ō

71. gehongne : *MS* gehongęne.
72. woniað : *MS* wuniað.

f.57a        hālge under heofonum    holtes frætwe,
             ne feallað þǣr on foldan    fealwe blōstman,
        75   wudubēama wlite,    ac þǣr wrǣtlīce
             on þām trēowum symle    telgan gehladene,
             ofett ednīwe    in ealle tīd
             on þām grǣswonge    grēne stondaþ,
             gehroden hyhtlīce    Hāliges meahtum
        80   beorhtast bearwa.    Nō gebrocen weorþeð
             holt on hīwe.    Þǣr se hālga stenc
             wunaþ geond wynlond.    Þæt onwended ne bið
             ǣfre tō ealdre,    ǣrþon endige
             frōd fyrngeweorc    sē hit on frymþe gescōp.
        85   Ðone wudu weardaþ    wundrum fæger
             fugel feþrum strong,    sē is fenix hāten.
             Þǣr se ānhaga    eard bihealdeþ,
             dēormōd drohtað ;    nǣfre him dēaþ sceþeð
             on þām willwonge    þenden woruld stondeþ.
        90   Sē sceal þǣre sunnan    sīð behealdan
             ond ongēan cuman    Godes condelle,
             glædum gimme,    georne bewitigan
             hwonne ūp cyme    æþelast tungla,
             ofer ȳðmere    ēstan līxan
        95   Fæder fyrngeweorc,    frætwum blīcan
             torht tācen Godes.    Tungol bēoþ āhȳded,
             gewiten under waþeman    westdǣlas on,
             bidēglad on dægrēd    ond sēo deorce niht
             won gewīteð.    Þonne wāþum strong
       100   fugel feþrum wlonc    on firgenstrēam
             under lyft ofer lagu    lōcað georne
             hwonne ūp cyme    ēastan glīdan
             ofer sīðne sǣ    swegles lēoma.
             Swā se æþela fugel    æt þām ǣspringe
       105   wlitigfæst wunað    wyllestrēamas.
             Þǣr se tīrēadga    twelf sīþum hine
f.57b        bibaþað in þām burnan    ǣr þæs bēacnes cyme,
             sweglcondelle,    ond symle swā oft
             of þām wilsuman    wyllgespryngum
       110   brimcald beorgeð    æt baða gehwylcum.

    108. sweglcondelle : *MS* swel condelle *with* g *crowded in.*

Siþþan hine sylfne   æfter sundplegan
hēahmōd hefeð   on hēanne bēam,
þonan ȳþast mæg   on ēastwegum
sīð bihealdan   hwonne swegles tapur,
115 ofer holmþræce   hædre blīce
lēohtes lēoma.  Lond bēoð gefrætwad,
woruld gewlitegad,  siþþan wuldres gim,
ofer geofones gong   grund gescīneþ
geond middangeard   mærost tungla.
120    Sōna swā sēo sunne   sealte strēamas
hēa oferhlīfað,   swā se haswa fugel
beorht of þæs bearwes   bēame gewīteð,
fareð feþrum snell   flyhte on lyfte,
swinsað ond singeð   swegle tōhēanes.
125 Ðonne bið swā fæger   fugles gebæru,
onbryrded brēostsefa   blissum rēmig;
wrixleð wōðcræfte,   wundorlīcor
beorhtan reorde   þonne æfre byre monnes
hȳrde under heofonum,   siþþan Hēahcyning,
130 wuldres Wyrhta   woruld staþelode,
heofon ond eorþan.  Biþ þæs hlēoðres swēg
eallum songcræftum  swētra ond wlitigra
ond wynsumra   wrenca gehwylcum ;
ne magon þām breahtme   bȳman ne hornas
135 ne hearpan hlyn   ne hæleþa stefn
ænges on eorþan   ne organan,
swēglēoþres geswin   ne swanes feðre
ne ænig þāra drēama   þe Dryhten gescōp
gumum tō glīwe   in þās gēomran woruld.
140 Singeð swā ond swinsað   sælum geblissad
f.58a oþþæt sēo sunne   on sūðrodor
sæged weorþeð.  Þonne swīað hē
ond hlyst gefēð,  hēafde onbrygdeð
þrīst þonces glēaw,   ond þriwa āscæceð
145 feþre flyhthwate :  fugol bið geswiged.
Symle hē twelf sīþum   tīda gemearcað

---

115. holmþræce : *MS* holm wræce.

133. wynsumra : *MS* winsumra.

dæges ond nihtes.
        Swā gedēmed is
bearwes bīgenga   þæt hē þǣr brūcan mōt
wonges mid willum   ond welan nēotan,
150 līfes ond lissa,   londes frætwa,
oþþæt hē þūsende   þisses līfes,
wudubearwes weard,   wintra gebīdeþ.
Ðonne bið gehefgad   haswigfeðra
gomol gēarum frōd.   Grēne eorðan,
155 āflȳhð fugla wyn   foldan geblōwene
ond þonne gesēceð   sīde rīce
middangeardes,   þǣr nō men būgað,
eard ond ēþel.   Þǣr hē ealdordōm
onfēhð foremihtig   ofer fugla cynn
160 geþungen on þēode,   ond þrāge mid him
wēsten weardað.   Þonne wāþum strong
west gewīteð   wintrum gebysgad
flēogan feþrum snel.   Fuglas þringað
ūtan ymbe æþelne :   æghwylc wille
165 wesan þegn ond þēow   þēodne mǣrum
oþþæt hȳ gesēcað   Syrwara lond
corðra mǣste.   Him se clǣna þǣr
oðscūfeð scearplīce   þæt hē in scade weardað
on wudubearwe   wēste stōwe
170 biholene ond bihȳdde   hæleþa monegum.
Ðǣr hē hēanne bēam   on holtwuda
wunað ond weardað   wyrtum fæstne
under heofumhrōfe,   þone hātað men
fenix on foldan   of þæs fugles noman.
f.58b 175 Hafað þām trēowe forgiefen   tīrmeahtig Cyning,
Meotud moncynnes,   mīne gefrǣge,
þæt sē āna is   ealra bēama
on eorðwege   ūplǣdendra
beorhtast geblōwen.   Ne mæg him bitres wiht

---

154. Grēne : *MS* rene.
155. wyn : *not in MS.*
156. sīde : *with* d *altered in MS from* ð.
157. nō men : *MS* nómen, *with* e *altered from* a *in MS.*
171. holtwuda : a *in MS altered from* u.

180 scyldum sceððan,   ac gescylded ā
    wunað ungewyrded   þenden woruld stondeð.
    Ðonne wind ligeð,   weder bið fæger,
    hlūttor heofones gim   hālig scīneð,
    bēoð wolcen tōwegen,   wætra þrȳþe
185 stille stondað,   biþ storma gehwylc
    āswefed under swegle,   sūþan blīceð
    wedercondel wearm,   weorodum lȳhteð,
    ðonne on þām telgum   timbran onginneð,
    nest gearwian.   Bið him nēod micel
190 þæt hē þā yldu   ofestum mōte
    þurh gewittes wylm   wendan tō līfe,
    feorg geong onfōn.   Þonne feor ond nēah
    þā swētestan   somnað ond gædrað
    wyrta wynsume   ond wudublēda
195 tō þām eardstede,   æþelstenca gehwone,
    wyrta wynsumra   þe Wuldorcyning,
    Fæder frymða gehwæs   ofer foldan gescōp
    tō indryhtum   ælda cynne
    swētes under swegle.   Þær hē sylf biereð
200 in þæt trēow innan   torhte frætwe ;
    þær se wilda fugel   in þām wēstenne
    ofer hēanne bēam   hūs getimbreð
    wlitig ond wynsum,   ond gewīcað þær
    sylf in þām solere,   ond ymbseteð ūtan
205 in þām lēafsceade   līc ond feþre
    on healfa gehwāre   hālgum stencum
    ond þām æþelestum   eorþan blēdum.
    Siteð sīþes fūs.   Þonne swegles gim,
f.59a   on sumeres tīd   sunne hātost
210 ofer sceadu scīneð   ond gesceapu drēogeð,
    woruld geondwlīteð,   þonne weorðeð his
    hūs onhæted   þurh hādor swegl.
    Wyrta wearmiað,   willsele stȳmeð
    swētum swæccum,   þonne on swole byrneð
215 þurh fȳres feng   fugel mid neste.
    Bǣl bið onǣled.   Þonne brond þeceð

----

197. gehwæs : *MS* gewæs, *with a small* h, *now erased or obliterated,*
*above the line between the* e *and* w.

heoredrēorges hūs,   hrēoh ōnetteð,
fealo līg feormað,   ond fenix byrneð
fyrngēarum frōd ;   þonne fȳr þigeð
220 lǣnne līchoman ;   līf bið on sīðe,
fǣges feorhhord,   þonne flǣsc ond bān
ādlēg ǣleð.   Hwæþre him eft cymeð
æfter fyrstmearce   feorh ednīwe,
siþþan þā yslan   eft onginnað
225 æfter līgþrǣce   lūcan tōgædre
geclungne tō clēowenne.   Þonne clǣne bið
beorhtast nesta,   bǣle forgrunden
heaþorōfes hof.   Hrā bið ācōlad,
bānfæt gebrocen   ond se bryne sweþrað.
230   Þonne of þām āde   æples gelīcnes
on þǣre ascan bið   eft gemēted,
of þām weaxeð wyrm   wundrum fæger,
swylce hē of ǣgerum,   ūt ālǣde
scīr of scylle.   Þonne on sceade weaxeð
235 þæt hē ǣrest bið   swylce earnes brid,
fæger fugeltimber ;   ðonne furþor gin
wrīdað on wynnum   þæt hē bið wæstmum gelīc
ealdum earne,   ond æfter þon
feþrum gefrætwad   swylc hē æt frymðe wæs
240 beorht geblōwen.   Þonne brǣd weorþeð
eal ednīwe   eft ācenned,
synnum āsundrad.   Sumes onlīce
swā mon tō ondleofne   eorðan wæsmas
on hærfeste,   hām gelǣdeð
f.59b 245 wiste wynsume   ǣr wintres cyme
on rypes tīman,   þȳ lǣs hī rēnes scūr
āwyrde under wolcnum ;   þǣr hī wraðe mētað,
fōdorþege gefēon   þonne forst ond snāw
mid ofermægne   eorþan þeccað
250 wintergewǣdum ;   of þām wæstmum sceal
eorla ēadwelan   eft ālǣdan
þurh cornes gecynd,   þe ǣr clǣne bið
sǣd onsāwen,   þonne sunnan glǣm,
on lenctenne   līfes tācen

240. weorþeð : *second* e *altered in MS from* a.

255  weceð woruldgestrēon   þæt þā wæstmas bēoð,
     þurh āgne gecynd   eft ācende
     foldan frætwe ;   swā se fugel weorþeð
     gomel æfter gēarum   geong ednīwe
     flǣsce bifongen.   Nō hē fōddor þigeð,
260  mete on moldan   nemne meledēawes
     dǣl gebyrge,   sē drēoseð oft
     æt middre nihte ;   bī þon se mōdga his
     feorh āfēdeð   oþþæt fyrngesetu,
     āgenne eard   eft gesēceð.
265     Þonne bið āweaxen   wyrtum in gemonge
     fugel feþrum deal ;   feorh bið nīwe
     geong geofona ful.   Þonne hē of grēote his
     līc leoþucræftig,   þæt ǣr līg fornōm,
     somnað swoles lāfe,   searwum gegædrað
270  bān gebrosnad   æfter bǣlþræce,
     ond þonne gebringeð   bān ond yslan,
     ādes lāfe   eft ætsomne,
     ond þonne þæt wælrēaf   wyrtum biteldeð
     fægre gefrætwed.   Ðonne āfȳsed bið
275  āgenne eard   eft tō sēcan.
     Þonne fōtum ymbfēhð,   fȳres lāfe
     clām biclyppeð   ond his cȳþþu eft,
     sunbeorht gesetu,   sēceð on wynnum
f.60a  ēadig ēþellond.   Eall bið genīwad
280  feorh ond feþerhoma   swā hē æt frymþe wæs
     þā hine ǣrest God   on þone æþelan wong
     sigorfæst sette.   Hē his sylfes þǣr
     bān gebringeð,   þā ǣr brondes wylm
     on beorhstede   bǣle forþylmde,
285  ascan tō ēacan.   Þonne eal geador
     bebyrgeð beaducræftig   bān ond yslan
     on þām ēalonde.   Bið him ednīwe
     þǣre sunnan þegn   þonne swegles lēoht,
     gimma gladost,   ofer garsecg ūp
290  æþeltungla wyn   ēastan līxeð.
        Is se fugel fæger   forweard hīwe,
     blēobrygdum fāg   ymb þā brēost foran.
     Is him þæt hēafod   hindan grēne

wrǣtlīce wrixleð   wurman geblonden.
295 Þonne is se finta   fægre gedǣled,
sum brūn sum basu   sum blācum splottum
searolīce beseted.   Sindon þā fiþru
hwīt hindanweard   ond se hals grēne
nioþoweard ond ufeweard   ond þæt nebb līxeð
300 swā glæs oþþe gim,   geaflas scȳne
innan ond ūtan.   Is sēo ēaggebyrd
stearc ond hīwe   stāne gelīcast,
gladum gimme,   þonne in goldfate
smiþa orþoncum   biseted weorþeð.
305 Is ymb þone swēoran,   swylce sunnan hring,
bēaga beorhtast   brogden feðrum.
Wrǣtlīc is sēo womb neoþan   wundrum fæger
scīr ond scȳne.   Is se scyld ufan
frætwum gefēged   ofer þæs fugles bæc.
310 Sindon þā scancan   scyllum biweaxen,
fealwe fōtas.   Se fugel is on hīwe
ǣghwæs ǣnlīc,   onlīcost pēan,
wynnum geweaxen   þæs gewritu secgað.
f.60b   Nis he hinderweard   ne hygegǣlsa,
315 swār ne swongor   swā sume fuglas,
þā þe late þurh lyft   lācað fiþrum ;
ac hē is snel ond swift   ond swīþe lēoht,
wlitig ond wynsum   wuldre gemearcad.
Ēce is se Æþeling   sē þe him þæt ēad gefeð.
320   Þonne hē gewīteð   wongas sēcan,
his ealdne eard   of þisse ēþeltyrf.
Swā se fugel flēogeð,   folcum oðēaweð,
mongum monna   geond middangeard,
þonne somniað   sūþan ond norþan,
325 ēastan ond westan   ēoredciestum,
farað feorran ond nēan   folca þrȳþum
þǣr hī scēawiaþ   Scyppendes giefe
fægre on þām fugle,   swā him æt fruman sette

306. brogden : *MS* bregden.
324. somniað : *MS* somnað.
325. ēastan : *a long descending stroke between* e *and* a.
327. scēawiaþ : *with* þ *altered from* n *in MS.*

    sigora Sōðcyning   sellīcran gecynd,
330 frætwe fægran   ofer fugla cyn.
    Ðonne wundriað   weras ofer eorþan
    wlite ond wæstma,   ond gewritu cȳþað,
    mundum mearciað   on marmstāne
    hwonne se dæg ond sēo tīd   dryhtum geēawe
335 frætwe flyhthwates.   Ðonne fugla cynn
    on healfa gehwōre   hēapum þringað,
    sīgað sīdwegum,   songe lofiað,
    mærað mōdigne   meaglum reordum
    ond swā þone hālgan   hringe beteldað
340 flyhte on lyfte ;   fenix biþ on middum
    þrēatum biþrungen.   Þēoda wlītað,
    wundrum wāfiað   hū sēo wilgedryht
    wildne weorþiað,   worn æfter ōþrum,
    cræftum cȳþað   ond for cyning mærað
345 lēofne lēodfruman,   lædað mid wynnum
    æþelne tō earde,   oþþæt se ānhoga
    oðflēogeð feþrum snel   þæt him gefylgan ne mæg
    drȳmendra gedryht,   þonne duguða wyn
    of þisse eorþan tyrf   ēþel sēceð.
f.61a 350 Swā se gesæliga   æfter swylthwīle
    his ealdcȳðþe,   eft genēosað
    fægre foldan.   Fugelas cyrrað
    from þām gūðfrecan   gēomormōde
    eft tō earde.   Þonne se æþeling bið
355 giong in geardum.   God āna wāt,
    Cyning ælmihtig   hū his gecynde bið,
    wīfhādes þe weres ;   þæt ne wāt ænig
    monna cynnes   būtan Meotod āna
    hū þā wīsan sind   wundorlīce,
360 fæger fyrngesceap   ymb þæs fugles gebyrd.
    Þær se ēadga mōt   eardes nēotan,
    wyllestrēama   wuduholtum in,
    wunian in wonge   oþþæt wintra bið
    þūsend urnen.   Þonne him weorþeð
365 ende līfes :   hine ād þeceð

---

333. marmstāne : *MS* męarm stane *with* r *partly erased.*
342. wāfiað : *MS* wefiað.

þurh æledfȳr.   Hwæþre eft cymeð
āweaht wrǣtlīce   wundrum tō līfe.
Forþon hē drūsende   dēað ne bisorgað,
sāre swyltcwale,   þe him symle wāt
370 æfter līgþræce   līf ednīwe,
feorh æfter fylle,   þonne fromlīce
þurh briddes hād   gebrēadad weorðeð
eft of ascan,   edgeong weseð
under swegles hlēo.   Bið him self gehwæðer
375 sunu ond swǣs fæder   ond symle ēac
eft yrfeweard   ealdre lāfe.
Forgeaf him se meahta   moncynnes Fruma
þæt hē swā wrǣtlīce   weorþan sceolde
eft þæt ilce   þæt hē ǣr þon wæs
380 feþrum bifongen,   þēah hine fȳr nime.
Swā þæt ēce līf   ēadigra gehwylc
æfter sārwræce   sylf gecēoseð
þurh deorcne dēað,   þæt hē Dryhtnes mōt
æfter gēardagum   geofona nēotan
f.61b 385 on sindrēamum   ond siþþan ā
wunian in worulde   weorca tō lēane.
Þisses fugles gecynd   fela gelīces
bī þām gecornum   Crīstes þegnum
bēacnað in burgum,   hū hī beorhtne gefēan
390 þurh Fæder fultum   on þās frēcnan tīd
healdaþ under heofonum   ond him hēanne blǣd
in þām ūplīcan   ēðle gestrȳnaþ.
Habbaþ wē geascad   þæt se Ælmihtiga
worhte wer ond wīf   þurh his wundra spēd
395 ond hī þā gesette   on þone sēlestan
foldan scēates,   þone fīra bearn
nemnað neorxnawong,   þǣr him nǣnges wæs
ēades onsȳn,   þenden Ēces word,
Hālges hlēoþorcwide   healdan woldan
400 on þām nīwan gefēan.   Þǣr him nīþ gescōd,
ealdfēondes æfēst,   sē him ǣt gebēad,

371. fylle : *MS* fílle.
393. geascad : d *altered from* ð *in MS.*

P.—E

bēames blēde,  þæt hī bū þēgun
æppel unrǣdum  ofer ēst Godes,
byrgdon forbodene :  þǣr him bitter wearð
405 yrmþu æfter ǣte  ond hyra eaferum swā,
sārlīc symbel  sunum ond dohtrum.
Wurdon tēonlīce  tōþas īdge
āgolden æfter gylte.  Hæfdon Godes yrre,
bittre bealosorge.  Þæs þā byre siþþan
410 gyrne onguldon,  þe hī þæt gyfl þēgun
ofer Ēces word.  Forþon hȳ ēðles wyn
gēomormōde  ofgiefan sceoldon
þurh nǣdran nīþ,  þā hēo nearwe biswāc
yldran ūsse  in ǣrdagum
415 þurh fǣcne ferð,  þæt hī feor þonan
in þās dēaðdene  drohtað sōhton,
sorgfulran gesetu.  Him wearð sēlle līf
heolstre bihȳded  ond se hālga wong
þurh fēondes searo  fæste bitȳned
f.62a 420 wintra mengu,  oþþæt Wuldorcyning,
þurh His hidercyme  hālgum tōhēanes
moncynnes Gefēa,  mēþra Frēfrend
ond se ānga Hyht  eft ontȳnde.

Is þon gelīcast,  þæs þe ūs leorneras
425 weordum secgað  ond writu cȳþað,
þisses fugles gefær,  þonne frōd ofgiefeð
eard ond ēþel  ond geealdad bið,
gewīteð wērigmōd  wintrum gebysgad;
þær hē holtes hlēo  hēah gemēteð
430 in þām hē getimbreð  tānum ond wyrtum
þām æþelestum  eardwīc nīwe,
nest on bearwe;  bið him nēod micel
þæt hē feorh geong eft,  onfōn mōte
þurh līges blǣst  līf æfter dēaþe,
435 edgeong wesan  ond his ealdcȳðþu,
sunbeorht gesetu  sēcan mōte
æfter fȳrbaðe;  swā ðā foregengan,
yldran ūsse  ānforlēton

407. wurdon : *MS* wordon, *with first* o *reformed to* u.
408. āgolden : *MS* ageald.

þone wlitigan wong   ond wuldres setl
440 lēoflīc on lāste,   tugon longne sīð
in hearmra hond   þǣr him hettende,
earme āglǣcan   oft gescōdan.
Wǣron hwæþre monge   þā þe Meotude wel
gehȳrdun under heofonum   hālgum ðēawum,
445 dǣdum dōmlīcum,   þæt him Dryhten wearð,
heofona Hēahcyning   hold on mōde.
Ðæt is se hēa bēam   in þām hālge nū
wīc weardiað   þǣr him wihte ne mæg
ealdfēonda nān   ātre sceþþan,
450 fācnes tācne   on þā frēcnan tīd.
þǣr him nest wyrceð   wið nīþa gehwām
dǣdum dōmlīcum   Dryhtnes cempa,
f.62b   þonne hē ælmessan   earmum dǣleð,
dugeþa lēasum   ond him Dryhten gecȳgð,
455 Fæder on fultum,   forð ōnetteð,
lǣnan līfes   leahtras dwǣsceþ,
mirce māndǣde,   healdeð Meotudes ǣ
beald in brēostum   ond gebedu sēceð
clǣnum gehygdum   ond his cnēo bīgeð
460 æþele tō eorþan,   flȳhð yfla gehwylc,
grimme gieltas   for Godes egsan,
glædmōd gyrneð   þæt hē gōdra mǣst
dǣda gefremme ;   þām biþ Dryhten scyld,
in sīþa gehwane   sigora Waldend,
465 weoruda Wilgiefa.   Þis þā wyrta sind,
wæstma blēde   þā se wilda fugel
somnað under swegle   sīde ond wīde
tō his wīcstōwe,   þǣr hē wundrum fæst
wið nīþa gehwām   nest gewyrceð.
470 Swā nū in þām wīcum   willan fremmað,
mōde ond mægne   Meotudes cempan
mǣrða tilgað ;   þæs him meorde wile
Ēce ælmihtig   ēadge forgildan.
Bēoð him of þām wyrtum   wīc gestaþelad
475 in wuldres byrig   weorca tō lēane,
þæs þe hī gehēoldan   hālge lāre

443. wel : *MS* we.

　　　hāte æt eortan.　Hige weallende
　　　dæges ond nihtes　Dryhten lufiað,
　　　lēohte gelēafan　Lēofne cēosað
480　ofer woruldwelan ;　ne biþ him wynne hyht
　　　þæt hȳ þis lǣne līf　long gewunien.
　　　Þus ēadig eorl　ēcan drēames,
　　　heofona hāmes　mid Hēahcyning
　　　earnað on elne,　oþþæt ende cymeð
485　dōgorrīmes　þonne dēað nimeð,
　　　wiga wælgīfre　wǣpnum geþrȳþed
　　　ealdor ānra gehwæs　ond in eorþan fæðm

f.63a　snūde sendað　sāwlum binumene
　　　lǣne līchoman,　þǣr hī longe bēoð
490　oð fȳres cyme　foldan biþeahte.
　　　　Ðonne monge bēoð　on gemōt lǣdaþ
　　　fȳra cynnes :　wile Fæder engla,
　　　sigora Sōðcyning　seonoþ gehēgan,
　　　duguða Dryhten　dēman mid ryhte.
495　Þonne ǣriste　ealle gefremmaþ
　　　men on moldan,　swā se mihtiga Cyning,
　　　bēodeð Brego engla,　bȳman stefne
　　　ofer sīdne grund　sāwla Nergend.
　　　Bið se deorca dēað　Dryhtnes meahtum
500　ēadgum geendad.　Æðele hweorfað,
　　　þrēatum þringað,　þonne þēos woruld
　　　scyldwyrcende　in scome byrneð
　　　āde onǣled.　Weorþeð ānra gehwylc
　　　forht on ferþþe　þonne fȳr briceð
505　lǣne londwelan,　līg eal þigeð
　　　eorðan ǣhtgestrēon,　æpplede gold
　　　gīfre forgrīpeð,　grǣdig swelgeð
　　　londes frætwe.　Þonne on lēoht cymeð
　　　ældum þisses　in þā openan tīd
510　fæger ond gefēalīc　fugles tācen,
　　　þonne anwald eal　ūp āstellað,
　　　of byrgenum　bān gegædrað,
　　　leomu līc somod　ond līfes gǣst

512. gegædrað : *in MS an erasure after* ge.
513. līfes : *MS* liges.

fore Crīstes cnēo.  Cyning þrymlīce,
515 of his hēahsetle  hālgum scīneð
wlitig wuldres gim.  Wel biþ þām þe mōt
in þā gēomran tīd  Gode līcian.
    Ðǣr þā līchoman  leahtra clǣne
gongað glædmōde,  gǣstas hweorfað
520 in bānfatu  þonne bryne stīgeð
hēah tō heofonum.  Hāt bið monegum

f.63b    egeslīc ǣled  þonne ānra gehwylc
sōðfæst ge synnig,  sāwel mid līce
from moldgrafum  sēceð Meotudes dōm
525 forhtāfǣred.  Fȳr bið on tihte,
ǣleð uncyste.  Þǣr þā ēadgan bēoð
æfter wræchwīle  weorcum bifongen,
āgnum dǣdum.  Þæt þā æþelan sind
wyrta wynsume  mid þām se wilda fugel
530 his sylfes nest  biseteð ūtan,
þæt hit fǣringa  fȳre byrneð,
forsweleð under sunnan  ond hē sylfa mid,
ond þonne æfter līge  līf eft onfēhð
ednīwinga.  Swā bið ānra gehwylc
535 flǣsce bifongen  fīra cynnes
ǣnlīc ond edgeong,  sē þe his āgnum hēr
willum gewyrceð  þæt him Wuldorcyning
meahtig æt þām mæþle  milde geweorþeð.
    Þonne hlēoþriað  hālge gǣstas,
540 sāwla sōðfæste  song āhebbað
clǣne ond gecorene,  hergað Cyninges þrym
stefn æfter stefne,  stīgað tō wuldre
wlitige gewyrtad  mid hyra weldǣdum.
Bēoð þonne āmerede  monna gǣstas,
545 beorhte ābȳwde  þurh bryne fȳres.
    Ne wēne þæs ǣnig  ælda cynnes
þæt ic lygewordum  lēoð somnige,
wrīte wōðcræfte.  Gehȳrað wītedōm,
Iōbes gieddinga.  Þurh Gǣstes blǣd
550 brēostum onbryrded  beald reordade,
wuldre geweorðad  hē þæt word gecwæð :
' Ic þæt ne forhycge  heortan geþoncum

þæt ic in mīnum neste    nēobed cēose,
hæle hrāwērig,    gewīte hēan þonan

555 on longne sīð    lāme bitolden
geōmor gūdǣda    in grēotes fæðm,
ond þonne æfter dēaþe    þurh Dryhtnes giefe
swā se fugel fenix    feorh ednīwe,
æfter ǣriste    āgan mōte

560 drēamas mid Dryhten,    þǣr sēo dēore scolu
Lēofne lofiað.    Ic þæs līfes ne mæg,
ǣfre tō ealdre    ende gebīdan
lēohtes ond lissa.    Þēah mīn līc scyle
on moldærne    molsnad weorþan

565 wyrmum tō willan,    swā þēah weoruda God
æfter swylthwīle    sāwle ālȳseð
ond in wuldor āweceð.    Mē þæs wēn nǣfre
forbirsteð in brēostum,    ðe ic in Brego engla
forðweardne gefēan    fæste hæbbe.'

570    Ðus frōd guma,    on fyrndagum
gieddade glēawmōd    Godes spelboda
ymb his ǣriste    in ēce līf
þæt wē þȳ geornor    ongietan meahten
tīrfæst tācen    þæt se torhta fugel

575 þurh bryne bēacnað.    Bāna lāfe,
ascan ond yslan    ealle gesomnað
æfter līgbryne,    lǣdeþ siþþan
fugel on fōtum    tō Frēan geardum,
sunnan tōgēanes.    Þǣr hī siþþan forð

580 wuniað wintra fela,    wæstmum genīwad
ealles edgiong,    þǣr ǣnig ne mæg
in þām lēodscype    lǣþþum hwōpan.
Swā nū æfter dēaðe    þurh Dryhtnes miht
somod sīþiaþ    sāwla mid līce

585 fægre gefrætwed    fugle gelīcast
in ēadwelum    æþelum stencum,
þǣr sēo sōþfæste    sunne līhteð
wlitig ofer weoredum    in wuldres byrig.

Ðonne sōðfæstum    sāwlum scīneð

584. sīþiaþ : *final* þ *corrected in MS from* n.
586. ēadwelum : um *altered in MS from* an.

590 hēah ofer hrōfas    hǣlende Crīst.
 Him folgiað    fuglas scȳne,
 beorhte gebrēdade    blissum hrēmige
 in þām gladan hām    gǣstas gecorene
 ēce tō ealdre.    Þǣr him yfle ne mæg,
595 fāh fēond gemāh    fācne sceþþan,
 ac þǣr lifgað ā    lēohte werede,
 swā se fugel fenix,    in freoþu Dryhtnes
 wlitige in wuldre.    Weorc ānra gehwæs
 beorhte blīceð    in þām blīþam hām
600 fore onsȳne    ēcan Dryhtnes
 symle in sibbe    sunnan gelīce.
 Þǣr se beorhta bēag    brogden wundrum
 eorcnanstānum    ēadigra gehwām
 hlīfað ofer hēafde.    Heafelan līxað
605 þrymme biþeahte.    Ðēodnes cynegold
 sōðfæstra gehwone    sellīc glengeð
 lēohte in līfe,    þǣr se longa gefēa
 ēce ond edgeong    ǣfre ne sweþrað,
 ac hȳ in wlite wuniað    wuldre bitolden
610 fægrum frætwum    mid Fæder engla.
   Ne bið him on þām wīcum    wiht tō sorge,
 wrōht ne wēþel    ne gewindagas,
 hungor se hāta    ne se hearde þurst,
 yrmþu ne yldo.    Him se æþela Cyning
615 forgifeð gōda gehwylc.    Þǣr gǣsta gedryht
 Hǣlend hergað    ond Heofoncyninges
 meahte mǣrsiað,    singað Metude lof.
 Swinsað sibgedryht    swēga mǣste
 hǣdre ymb þæt hālge    hēahseld Godes,
620 blīþe blētsiað    Bregu sēlestan
 ēadge mid englum    efenhlēoþre þus :
 ' Sib sī Þē, sōð God,    ond snyttrucræft,
 ond Þē þonc sȳ    þrymsittendum
 geongra gyfena,    gōda gehwylces ;
625 micel unmǣte    mægnes strenðu
 hēah ond hālig.    Heofonas sindon
 fægre gefylled,    Fæder ælmihtig,
 ealra þrymma Þrym,    þīnes wuldres

uppe mid englum    ond on eorðan somod.
630 Gefreoþa ūsic, frymþa Scyppend ;  Þū eart Fæder
ælmihtig,
in hēannesse    heofuna Waldend.'
Đus reordiað    ryhtfremmende
mānes āmerede    in þære mæran byrig,
cyneþrym cȳþað,    Cāseres lof
635 singad on swegle,    sōðfæstra gedryht,
þām ānum is    ēce weorðmynd
forð būtan ende.    Næs his frymð æfre,
ēades ongyn.    Þēah hē on eorþan hēr
þurh cildes hād    cenned wære
640 in middangeard,    hwæþre his meahta spēd,
hēah ofer heofonum    hālig wunade
dōm unbryce.    Þēah hē dēaþes cwealm,
on rōde trēow    ræfnan sceolde
þearlīc wīte,    hē þȳ þriddan dæge
645 æfter līces hryre    līf eft onfēng
þurh Fæder fultum.    Swā fenix bēacnað
geong in geardum    Godbearnes meaht
þonne hē of ascan    eft onwæcned
in līfes līf    leomum geþungen.
650 Swā se Hǣlend ūs    elpe gefremede,
þurh his līces gedāl    līf būtan ende,
swā se fugel swētum    his fiþru tū
ond wynsumum    wyrtum gefylleð,
fægrum foldwæstmum    þonne āfȳsed bið.
655    Þæt sindon þā word,    swā ūs gewritu secgað,
f.65b    hlēoþor hāligra,    þe him tō heofonum bið,
tō þām mildan Gode    mōd āfȳsed
in drēama drēam,    þær hī Dryhtne tō giefe,
worda ond weorca    wynsumne stenc
660 in þā mæran gesceaft,    Meotude bringað
in þæt lēohte līf.    Sȳ Him lof symle
þurh woruld worulda    ond wuldres blǣd,
ār ond onwald    in þām ūplīcan
rodera rīce.    Hē is on ryht Cyning
665 middangeardes    ond mægenþrymmes
wuldre biwunden    in þære wlitigan byrig.

Hafað ūs ālȳfed    lucis auctor
þæt wē mōtun hēr    merueri,
gōddǣdum begietan    gaudia in celo,
670 þǣr wē mōtum    maxima regna
sēcan ond gesittan,    sedibus altis
lifgan in lisse    lucis et pacis,
āgan eardinga    alma letitię,
brūcan blǣddaga,    blandem et mittem
675 gesēon sigora Frēan    sine fine
ond Him lof singan    laude perenne
ēadge mid englum.    Alleluia.

667. auctor : *MS* a,ᵘctor.

# NOTES

1. The exordium is in full accord with Old English epic tradition and may be compared with the opening lines of *Beowulf*, *Andreas* and *Exodus*. The first six lines of the poem are compared in detail with the opening of the *Carmen* in 'The Form'. For a discussion of paradise see 'Paradise'.

2. **ēastdǣlum on**—the *Carmen* has *in primo oriente*. Paradise in the Christian tradition is particularly associated with the east, whereas the terrestrial paradise in classical authors is often in the west. Emerson, p. 21 (n.), suggests that, as the phoenix flies west to Syria, the Old English poet thought its home was in India, as in the Greek *Physiologus*. Yet not only are the poet's descriptions too imprecise for us to make any claims of this sort, but also such information as we have suggests that the phoenix's home was situated beyond the known human world. For *middangeard* in this poem is used of this world (cf. lines 4, 42, 119, 323, 640) and at lines 156-7 the phoenix is said to fly from his home to this world, *sīde rīce middangeardes*. This corresponds to the *Carmen's hunc orbem* (64) ; see Fitzpatrick's note to this line. And in these opening lines the phoenix's home is explicitly said to be situated far from man ; see further notes to lines 4, 6.

3. Both **folde** and *eorðe* are commonly linked with **scēat,** but normally *scēat* is in the plural number. Apart from the example at line 396, which is emended by most editors to the plural anyway (but see note to that line), this is the only example where *scēat* is used in the singular in this phrase. The plural has the sense of 'the whole of the earth' ; the sg. refers to a particular region of the world.

4. **ofer middangeard** modifies **mongum folcāgendra.** But it is disputed whether *mongum* means 'to many' or 'to everybody'. Schlotterose would accept the former as paradise is barred only to the wicked, and Emerson, p. 22 (n.), who likewise accepts this translation, thinks that there is a reference to the Biblical conception of paradise as the home of the lowly, rather than of those of high estate. But in a similar expression at line 323 *mongum monna geond middangeard* we are clearly to understand all men on earth, for the phoenix there symbolises Christ who is revealed to all men. Similarly *hæleþa monegum* (170) and *monge fȳra cynnes* (491-2) both mean the whole of the human race. So translate here 'to no one'.

5. Sweet's emendation of **folcāgendra** to *foldāgendra*, which is accepted by Bright, is unnecessary. The word *folcāgend* is also found at *Juliana* 186 and *Beowulf* 3113, whereas *foldāgend* is otherwise unknown. Although the original sense of *folcāgend* is 'ruler of a people, chieftain', it has here a more general sense of 'men'. In *Beowulf* the *folcāgende* are also referred to as *hæleða monegum*, *boldāgendra*.

6. The **mānfremmende** are the opposite of the *ryhtfremmende mānes āmerede* (632-3), who are said to be the inhabitants of paradise. There is confusion between the literal and allegorical levels here : the phoenix's home is far from all men, but the spiritual paradise is reserved for the blessed alone. This confusion between the story and the allegory occurs frequently in the poem, cf. lines 11-12, etc.

8. Scents play an important part in the poem. For a discussion of scents in the phoenix cult see Introduction, and of scents in Christian allegory see M. Laurent, 'Le phénix, les serpents et les aromates dans une miniature du XIIe siècle', *L'Antiquité Classique*, iv (1935), 375-401. Scented spices, especially myrrh (*chrisma*), played an important part in the baptismal service of the early church. Spices were smeared on the forehead, ears, nose and chest of the candidate for baptism and they were regarded as the material means used by the Holy Spirit for bringing heavenly gifts to the new Christian ; see St. Cyril of Jerusalem, *Catechesis* XXI, *Mystagogica* III, 4 (*Pat. Gr.* XXXIII, col. 1091-2). Regarded in this way, the scents are very appropriate in the phoenix myth, for the phoenix surrounded itself with them when about to embark on a new and purer life.

12. It has been suggested that **hlēoþra wyn** is a poor parallel to **heofonrīces duru**. Yet despite some editors' objections, it is quite satisfactory to read them as parallel, for it is not uncommon to find parallels built up of parts which are not real variants and which would hardly have been tolerated in the older poetry, cf. lines 75-8. Cook and Krapp-Dobbie think that *hlēoþra wyn* refers to the singing of the blessed, cf. lines 615-54. But in that case it is difficult to appreciate how the *ēadgum* 'to the blessed' is to be understood, since the poet can hardly have meant that the singing of the blessed was revealed to the blessed. It would be more appropriate to assume that the music refers to angelic choirs. The blessed in paradise (*ðǣr* 11) are entertained by the music of angelic choirs when the doors of heaven are opened. It is frequently stated that the inhabitants of paradise were regaled with beautiful music. If one interprets the lines in this way, we have another example of the allegory making itself manifest in the account of the phoenix, a common enough feature of the first half of the poem.

13. Most editors have a heavy stop after **roderum**. But Schlotterose has one after **wong** to create an object for *gewyrdan* (19) and to avoid having a plural *wealdas* parallel to a sg. *wong* and dependent upon *þæt is*. But parallels of different number are quite permissible, cf. lines 76-7, 233-4.

15. The implication of **fȳres blǣst,** for which there is no corresponding phrase in the *Carmen*, is that there is no excessive heat in paradise, just as there is no excessive cold. It is the constant change from hot to cold which is described as one of the principal torments of hell in *The Later Genesis*, and the poet of *The Phoenix* is no doubt indicating that this is not the case in heaven. At line 39,

however, the leaves on the trees in paradise are said not to be injured by fire, where in the corresponding passage the *Carmen* has a reference to Phaeton's chariot. Possibly the English poet had this reference in mind here as well and meant the *fȳres blǣst* to refer to the heat of the sun (cf. *sunnan hǣtu* 17), though fire to the Anglo-Saxon would normally imply either Doomsday (cf. *līges blǣst* 434) or hell. The use of rhyme should be noted in these lines.

19. The verb **gewyrdan** is generally transitive, but as *wihte* is an instrumental sg. meaning 'in any way', the verb lacks an object. Most editors accept an intransitive use of *gewyrdan* here and this is the most satisfactory solution.

25. Many early scholars, who relied on Sievers' five metrical types of an Old English poetic half-line, claimed that to derive **hleonað** from *hleonian, hlinian* 'to tower, lean', made line 25b metrically defective, and many emendations have been proposed. Apart from Bright's suggestion that 'the metre may be corrected by substituting an Anglian dissyllabic form of the personal ending' in *hleonað* (Third edition, 1894), the two major lines of approach are to posit a long diphthong for the verb or to read *ōo* as disyllabic. Editors, however, have not emended the text ; and there is no need to do so. Modern scholarship has shown that light verses with only one full stress are quite permissible in Old English poetry and line 25b can be interpreted metrically as x x x́ x x. See further A. J. Bliss, *The Metre of Beowulf*, 1958, pp. 61 ff. and references there. The verb *hleonian* 'to tower, lean' gives excellent sense here, and *ōo* is an acceptable orthographic variant of *ō* (cf. line 72), for long vowels are often doubled orthographically.

28. It is to be understood, of course, that this land is on a high mountain, the top of which is a kind of plateau and contains no rugged features. For **hęrra** Cook and Schlotterose read *hęrre* to agree with neuter *lond*. But *hęrra* could be taken as an orthographical variant of *hęrre*, which would agree with either *lond* (n) or *folde* (f) ; see 'Language' B (i).

28-30. The *Carmen* also has that the land was twelve cubits (*per bis sex ulnas*) higher than the highest mountain, a common feature in both classical and Christian accounts, see H. R. Patch, *The Other World*, 1950, p. 142. For the significance of the number twelve see *Dictionary of the Bible*, ed. J. Hastings, III, p. 563 ; and for a typical medieval interpretation of twelve see Rabanus Maurus, *De Universo* XVIII. 3 (*Pat. Lat.* CXI, col. 492). *PP* has that the Flood was forty fathoms above the highest terrestrial mountain and paradise was another forty fathoms above this. The reference to the wise men is merely a cliché here ; for similar expressions cf. lines 313, 424-5, 655.

36. E. von Schaubert, *Philologica*, 1949, pp. 33-4, suggests on the parallel of lines 79-80 that **swā** has a causal sense here and she translates 'sondern diese Bäume stehen immer grün da, weil Gott es ihnen gebot'. But perhaps a modal sense is more likely.

37. The poet has forgotten that there is neither summer nor winter in paradise.

39. The *Carmen*, lines 11-12, states that the phoenix's home remained inviolate when the rest of the world was engulfed by the flames from Phaeton's chariot. The Old English poet possibly refers to this here, though fire is a well-known feature of Doomsday, cf. lines 47, 490, 501-3, 521-2, and the mention of fire leads him on to look forward to Doomsday, lines 40-9. But the exclusion of Phaeton and Deucalion makes the change from the fire to the flood very abrupt.

41. **Swā** means 'when' here ; cf. the *Carmen's cum* and see BT s.v. *swā* V (8). The flood mentioned in the Latin is Deucalion's flood, but no doubt the English poet had the Biblical flood in mind. It is *Noes flōd* which is mentioned in *PP*. On lines 41-9 see further C. W. Kennedy, *The Earliest English Poetry*, 1943, pp. 291-2.

52. **Enge** means 'narrow', but Cook on account of the *Carmen's mors crudelis* glossed it as 'cruel'. *Enge* is commonly associated with hell in Old English poetry, cf. *Genesis* 356, *Solomon and Saturn* 106, and it is not unlikely that the idea of 'narrow confinement' should have been extended to death itself.

53. Hall translates **lāþes cyme** as 'the loathed foe's coming', taking *lāþes* from the adj. *lāþ*. But most editors understand it as the genitive of the neuter noun with the abstract sense of 'harm, evil', cf. Gollancz's 'nor harm's approach'. Either translation is possible. It can be said of the latter that as the list of what is excluded is largely made up of abstracts, *lāþes* is more appropriately understood as an abstract. But as the absence of a *lāðgeniðla* (50) is mentioned, the former is just as likely and makes excellent sense here. From this paradise even the devil is excluded, cf. lines 448-9.

55. Because of the *Carmen's cupido* (17), Thorpe translated **onsȳn** as 'desire'. But the Latin of the *Carmen* is not always an authoritative guide to the meaning of the Old English. As *swā eorðan bið ansȳn wæteres* (Psalm cxlii, 6) corresponds to the Vulgate *sicut terra sine aqua*, it is better to translate *onsȳn* as 'lack, absence'. For there being no lack of wealth in paradise, cf. *Genesis* ii, 12.

56. **Ne sorg ne slǣp** hardly corresponds to the *Carmen's et curae insomnes* (20), though Richmond, p. 11, suggests that the English poet had a MS with a reading *aut curae in somnis*. But Cook, *MLN*, xiv (1899), 450-1, defended the MS reading, noting the connexion between sorrow and sleep in *The Wanderer* 39-40, *Crist* 1661 and *Solomon and Saturn* 313. There seems to be no particular reason, except perhaps alliteration, why sorrow and sleep are closely connected in Old English ; though in the Vulgate one finds the disciples *dormientes prae tristitia* (Luke xxii. 45). Sorrow and sleep are also excluded from paradise in St. Audoenus' *Life of St. Eligius*, see N. Blake, 'Originality in "The Phoenix" ', *NQ*, ccvi (1961), 326-7. It is understandable that sorrow should be excluded from paradise, but sleep was probably thought of as not

being present on account of its association with sloth and on account of the absence of night in paradise. The absence of sleep is also mentioned in *The Judgement Day II* 258; the absence of night and sorrow being mentioned in the same passage.

62-4. It is best to take **wyllan** as nom. pl. of *wylla* 'a well' and parallel to *lagustrēamas*, as most editors do. Most editors have accepted Grein's emendation of **foldwylmum** to *flōdwylmum*. The presence of *foldan* (64b) and the occurrence of the interchange of *lo/ol* in the MS, cf. *Riddle* 15/9, *Judgement Day I* 23, make this a tempting emendation. Furthermore *flōdwylm* is found at *Andreas* 516, though there are no other examples of *foldwylm*; and the element *flōd-* repeats the idea of *lagu-* (62). But *foldwylm* makes excellent sense here and there seems to be no good reason why it should be emended out of existence.

72. Most editors emend *wuniað* to *waniað* after Thorpe, though Krapp-Dobbie say 'there is no real objection to the MS reading'. But as *a* plus nasal appears as *o* in the Exeter Book, perhaps *woniað* is a better emendation; cf. *woniað* (*Crist* 951).

75 ff. This passage has been the subject of much discussion and emendation because of the paucity of verbs and the problem of what the one verb *stondaþ* agrees with. Many earlier editors had a full stop after *tīd* (77) and started a new sentence at *on þām græswonge*, which left the *ac* clause (75b-77) without a verb. This lack of a verb in lines 75b-77 was overcome by inserting *bēoð* between *þǣr* and *wrǣtlīce*; or by emending *symle* to *syndon*, although *symle* is parallel to *in ealle tīd*; or by understanding a part of the verb 'to be'. Krapp-Dobbie, however, have a full stop at *frætwe* (73) with no stop after *tīd*; but this destroys the style of the passage with a negation *þǣr nō* (72) balanced by an affirmation *ac þǣr* (75); cf. *þǣr ne* (60) . . . *ac þǣr* (62). E. von Schaubert, *Philologica*, 1949, pp. 31 ff., has shown that the final clause (79-80a) is an absolute participial construction in the nominative which she translates in a causal sense. We can therefore accept with Krapp-Dobbie that *telgan* and *ofett ednīwe* are parallel and together form the subject of *stondaþ*. For the parallelism of a plural with a singular phrase cf. lines 13, 233-4. The passage could be translated along these lines : 'but there gloriously the new fruit, the laden branches remain forever throughout eternity in bloom on the trees in that grassy plain, because the brightest of groves is joyfully decked through the might of the Holy One'.

87. The word **ānhaga** (also at line 346) translates the Latin *unica* (31), with which cf. Ovid's phoenix *unica semper avis* (*Amores* II, vi, 54); see further Fitzpatrick, p. 67. No doubt the poet meant the word *ānhaga* to have the sense of 'uniqueness', and Gollancz's translation 'lonely' goes against the interpretation of the whole poem, for neither the phoenix nor any of its allegorical equivalents is lonely. Possibly the poet here drew a connexion between *ānhaga* and *ǣnlīc*, used both of the phoenix and its home (9, 312).

88. Gollancz translates **dēormōd drohtaδ** as 'its brave existence'. But *dēormōd* cannot agree with accusative masculine *drohtaδ*. Bright, Hall and Cook take *drohtaδ* as the 3 sg. pres. of the verb *drohtian* 'to dwell, live'. Schlotterose (after Trautmann) has it as a noun, but takes *dēormōd* to agree with the phoenix (*se ānhaga*) and translates : 'dort hat der kühngesinnte aufenthalt'. This is accepted by Krapp-Dobbie, who note the occurrence of the noun *drohtaδ* at 416. Either interpretation is possible, but perhaps Schlotterose's is preferable.

90. Emerson, pp. 20-1, claimed that the English poet omitted all reference to the phoenix's relation to the sun myth. But this is surely to misunderstand the nature of the poem. Many of the phoenix's actions are dependent on the sun, the phoenix waits in impatience for the sun to appear (113-16), it sings while the sun is in the heavens and is silent as soon as the sun sets (124, 141-3). The phoenix is subservient to the sun. The poet has kept this relationship between the phoenix and the sun because of the allegorical interpretation, for Christ is symbolised by the sun and the blessed by the phoenix.

103. For **sīône** cf. eOE *sīdne* ; see 'Language' C (iii) a.

104. The **ǣspring** is to be equated with the *fons* in the *Carmen*, *quem 'vivum' nomine dicunt* (25). In *PP* the phoenix bathes *on pǣre līfes welle.*

110. Kock, *Jubilee Jaunts and Jottings*, 1918, pp. 59-60, takes **brimcald** as an uninflected adj. agreeing with *wyllgespryngum*, but it is better to take it as acc. sg. n. agreeing with *wæter* understood.

121. For **haswa** cf. *haswigfeδra* (153). The word is also used of the eagle (*Riddle* 24/4), the dove (*Genesis* 1451) and smoke (*Riddle* 1/7). *Haswa* probably refers to a pale-grey colour and may well be a traditional epithet, as Cook suggests. ON *hoss* is used of the wolf and eagle ; OHG *hasan* has the sense 'bright, white' ; and MHG *haswe* means 'pale, wan'. See further M. Trautmann, 'Hasu', *BBA*, xix (1905), 216-18.

123. The phoenix is no doubt described as fleet of wing, for it is distinguished from those birds which are sluggish and slow of flight (314-16). So the blessed are eager to seek their salvation, unlike those who drag their feet in this matter.

124. For **tōhēanes** cf. line 421 and see 'Language' C (ii).

125. **Swā** is intensive here ; translate 'very, exceedingly' ; cf. BT s.v. *swā* IV (4). **Gebǣru** is generally glossed 'bearing, behaviour'; Gollancz, for example, translates here 'the bearing of the bird'. But the meaning 'outcry, clamour' is more suitable in the Anglo-Saxon Chronicle 755, possibly at *Elene* 709-10, and in Middle English *ibere* has the sense 'voice' in *The Owl and the Nightingale* 222. The meaning 'voice, song' seems best here, as was suggested by Hall, p. 23, n. 2. If *gebǣru* is interpreted in this way, then lines 125-6 harmonise better with the preceding and following lines. The *onbryrded brēostsefa* (126) will mean that the phoenix's heart was

inspired to song, cf. *brēostum onbryrded beald reordade* (550). The phoenix's song corresponds to both the singing of the blessed in paradise and the prophecy by Job.

126. For **rēmig** cf. eOE *hrĕmig* and see 'Language' C (i) a. As it stands *rēmig* agrees with *brēostsefa*, though it would perhaps be more satisfactory if it were understood to refer to the phoenix itself. Cf. line 592 where the blessed are said to be *blissum hrēmige*.

134. The infinitive 'equal' can be understood to be omitted here ; cf. Thorpe's translation : 'that sound may not equal trumpets nor horns'. For *bȳman* and *hornas* see F. M. Padelford, *Old English Musical Terms*, 1899, pp. 54-6.

136b-137a. These two half-lines have caused difficulty because of the uncertainty of the meaning of *organan* and *swēglēopres*. For the form of the latter see 'Language' C (i) a. Grundtvig and others put *swēg* at the end of line 136, and Thorpe and Gollancz translate 'nor organ's tone'. But the compound *swēghlēopor* is found at *The Panther* 42 and seems appropriate here, cf. line 131. Cook omits a comma after *organan* and translates 'the strain of the organ's melody'. But *swēglēopres geswin*, 'the strain of harmony', gives adequate sense by itself, and it is more probable that *organan* is a nom. pl. parallel to *bȳman* and *hornas*. F. M. Padelford, *Old English Musical Terms*, 1899, p. 86, discriminates between OE *organ* 'a song, canticle, a song with vocal accompaniment' and OE *organa ?*, *organe ?* 'a musical instrument, a pipe organ'. Although either sense would be applicable here, we have surely to deal with the latter. The gender of the word is uncertain, though J. B. Bessinger, *A Short Dictionary of Anglo-Saxon Poetry*, glosses the word under *organan f. pl.* Latin *organum* could refer to any musical instrument : *organa dicuntur omnia instrumenta musicorum* (*Pat. Lat.* XXXVI, col. 671). But here we should no doubt understand some sort of pipe organ. Although the earliest organs were nothing more than a rude set of pipes bound together, by the time of Tertullian hydraulic and pneumatic organs were known. See further Padelford, *op. cit.*, pp. 25, 43-9.

137b. The *Carmen* has *olor moriens* (49). *Riddle* 7, which is widely accepted as referring to a swan, has :

> Frætwe mīne
> swōgað hlūde   ond swinsiað,
> torhte singað,   þonne ic getenge ne bēom
> flōde ond foldan,   fērende gǣst.   (6-9)

So by **swanes feðre** we may understand the noise made by the swan's wings in flight.

144. Because *ter* is repeated in the *Carmen*, lines 53-4, Schlotterose and Cook emend **prīst** to *priwa*. But this repetition need not have been carried over to the Old English and *prīst* makes good sense. For *āscæceð fepre flyhthwate* the *Carmen* has *alarum repetito verbere plaudit* (53). Cook notes that the flapping of the phoenix's wings

(i.e. beating its breast) is generally associated with the lighting of the pyre ; cf. Isidore's *et conversa ad radium solis alarum plausu voluntarium sibi incendium nutrit* (*Pat. Lat.* LXXXII, col. 462).

148. **Bīgenga** is the dat. without final *n* ; see 'Language' C (vi) b and Cosijn, *Beitr.*, xxiii (1898), 121.

151. F. A. Blackburn, *MLN*, x (1895), 259-60, has suggested that **pūsende** is possibly a ja-stem noun and he compared *hǣlende* (590) beside normal *hǣlend*, where the final *e* is demanded by the metre.

153. The context shows that **gehefgad** means 'weighed down (by age)' rather than 'sad, depressed' ; cf. *wintrum gebysgad* (162). For **haswigfeðra** cf. *se haswa fugel* (121).

155. Grein's emendation to **fugla wyn(n)** is now generally accepted, for *wyn* is used frequently with a preceding gen. in *The Phoenix*, e.g. lines 12, 70, 290, 348, 411. The only possible objection is that *fugles wyn* is used of a quill in *Riddle* 26 ; but this is not an important objection as the form is there in the gen. sg.

158 ff. In the *Carmen* the phoenix flies direct from its home to Syria. But the English poet has divided the journey into two stages ; from the phoenix's home to an uninhabited spot in this world (156-8), although there is no indication where this might be, and from there westwards to Syria (161-7).

166. The plural **hȳ**, which some editors emend to *hē*, can be kept as referring to the phoenix together with the other birds. **Corðra mǣste** will then be translated 'in a large band', cf. *lēohte werede* (596) and *mid corðre* (*Andreas* 1075).

168. **Sc(e)ad** occurs several times in the poem, cf. lines 210, 234 and 205 (*lēafscead*). The normal meaning of the word is 'shadow' as at line 210. But as the *Carmen* has *secretosque petit deserta per avia lucos* (67), it is possible that *in scade* here means 'in a secret shelter, refuge' ; cf. *on ðām sceade his geteldes : in abscondito tabernaculi sui* (quoted in BT s.v. *scead*). **Wēste** (169) means 'waste, uncultivated, deserted', and in the Old English glosses it normally glosses Latin *desertus*. Perhaps the English poet has unconsciously transposed the Latin epithets, applying *deserta* to the place inhabited and *secretos* to its location. Translate : 'so that he inhabits a desolate spot in a refuge in a grove'.

173. For **heofumhrōfe** cf. eOE *heofonhrōfe* and see 'Language' C (vi) a.

174. In the *Carmen* the tree is a palm, which is the tree usually connected with the phoenix. It is only in the *Carmen* and *The Phoenix* that the tree is named after the bird ; in other sources the bird is named after the tree, cf. Isidore's *Etymologiarum*, XVII, vii, 1 (*Pat. Lat.* LXXXII, col. 609).

179 f. The **him** must refer to the phoenix who is safe from all dangers in the security of the palm tree, as the blessed are safe in the embrace of Christ, cf. lines 448-50. The *Carmen*, lines 71-2, also has that the phoenix was safe in the palm tree. But in the Old English the passage is very closely related to lines 448-50 and 594-5, which

give the allegorical interpretation. The phoenix in the palm is safe from all evil which could be inflicted by the devil, just as the blessed in heaven are safe from the attentions of the devil. These passages give support to Tupper's translation of lines 179-80 : 'nor does aught that is grievous hurt him with evils' (*PMLA*, xxv (1910), 173).

191. **Wylm,** which normally refers to the surging of fire or water, has the sense of 'passionate excitement' when applied to the human or animal spirit ; cf. *brēostwylm* (*Beowulf* 1877), *hygewælm* (*Genesis* 980). The phoenix wishes to change its old life for the new one, just as, the allegory implies, the Christian wishes to change the old life of sin for the new life in Christ ; cf. Ambrose's *Hexameron* V, 80, Appendix I (b). Cosijn, Beitr., xxiii (1898), 122, compares *wielm ðæs mōdes* translating *frixura mentis* (*Cura Pastoralis*, ed. H. Sweet, EETS Original Series 45, pp. 162-3), and so translates 'brand, durch seine Vernunft, d.h. vernünftig, klug gestiftet'. Tupper, *PMLA*, xxv (1910), 173, translates 'through ardor (or "labor") of spirit'. Gollancz and Thorpe take *gewitt* as 'knowledge', and Cook translates the phrase 'through perturbation of spirit, through excitement of mind'. Not only is *gewitt* the home of the emotional as well as the rational faculties, cf. *weallende gewitt* (*Elene* 937), but a translation should also imply the allegorical interpretation. A suitable translation might be 'through passionate desire of the spirit'.

192. **Feorg geong** must be read as two words, *feorg* being the object of *onfōn* ; cf. *feorh bið nīwe geong* (266-7).

199. Gollancz, Schlotterose and Cook emend **swētes** to *swētest* ; but the other editors keep *swētes*, which can be regarded as an orthographical variant of *swētest* ; see 'Language' C (v). Krapp-Dobbie suggested that *swētes* was a gen. sg. 'of (what is) sweet under heaven' parallel to the genitives in lines 195-6 ; but this seems less probable.

202. Krapp-Dobbie's translation of **ofer hēanne bēam** as 'at the top of the tall tree' is better than Gollancz's 'on its lofty branches' ; cf. *ofer hēanne hrōf hand scēawedon* (*Beowulf* 983).

204. **Solere** is from Latin *solarium* 'a room open to the sun and receiving a lot of sunlight' ; cf. Old Saxon *soleri*, OHG *solari*. See further OED s.v. *sollar*. See also Blake, p. 54 (n.).

210. Cook takes the phoenix to be the subject of **drēogeð** and quotes *swā þēos woruld . . . gesceap drēogeð* (*Homiletic Fragment II*, 6-7). But it is better as other editors do to take the sun as the subject ; cf. Gollancz's translation : 'the sun . . . surveying all the world, fulfilleth fate's decree'.

217. For **heoredrēorges** cf. eOE *heorodrēorges* ; see 'Language' B (i).

226. Gollancz, following Thorpe, translates **þonne clǣne bið** as 'when that brightest nest . . . becometh clean'. But it is better to take *clǣne* as an adv. 'entirely, wholly' here as the other editors do.

230. As early as Herodotus the ashes are said to have been moulded into a shape like a ball, but the comparison of this with

an apple may well be due to the Old English poet.

232. The worm is mentioned by Pliny and some of the early Christian authors, notably St. Clement the Roman ; see further 'The Development of the Phoenix Story'.

233. Schlotterose claimed that the dat.pl. **ǣgerum** must be incorrect here as we would have expected a dat.sg. parallel to *scylle*. He emended to *ǣgre* ; Thorpe and others to *ǣge*. But it is quite permissible to have parallels of different number, cf. lines 13, 76-7. A part of the verb 'to be' is to be understood with the *ālǣde* which here has an intransitive sense; cf. *ālǣdan* (251). The English poet did not follow the *Carmen* very closely here. The *Carmen* (101-4) states that there was first a milk-white worm which grew, then slept and then took on the appearance of an egg. Finally it burst through this covering. In *The Phoenix* we have first an apple-shaped ball, from which the worm appears like a chicken out of an egg. Herodotus is the only other author to mention an egg in connexion with the phoenix.

236a. Despite the fact that *magutimber* occurs three times in Old English, Schlotterose denied that it could be used to support the reading **fugeltimber**, for the former means 'kind, progeny', and the latter 'fledgeling'. He emended to *fugelumber*. But this is unnecessary and as Cook states *timber* means 'the material or substance of which a thing is made'. It is an adequate expression for the half-formed bird.

236b. In many early Christian works the phoenix after immolation is said to be restored to its former state in three days. Thus in the Greek *Physiologus* we read 'The next day the priest, upon examining the altar, finds a worm in the ashes. The second day it puts forth wings, and on the third it is restored to its former state.' (Quoted in Fitzpatrick, p. 81.) These three days symbolise the three days between Christ's death and resurrection. Cook suggested that three stages were to be found in *The Phoenix* : (i) *brid, fugeltimber* ; (ii) *gelīc ealdum earne* ; (iii) *swylc hē æt frymðe wæs*. But this is to neglect the first stage when the phoenix is still a worm (232-4), which in the Christian Latin authors always represents the first stage or day. *The Phoenix* has at least four stages for the rebirth of the phoenix (and it is quite possible to interpret lines 240-2 as a fifth), so any comparison with the three days of the Resurrection is impossible. In *PP* the phoenix is said to rise again *on þān þriddan dæge*.

240. The interpretation of **brǣd** is disputed. Emerson, p. 25 (n.), suggests that *brǣd* may be an Anglian form for *bred*, a form of *brid*, 'a bird'. He thinks that the interpretation 'bird' gives better sense in the context, for as the bird has already been described as covered with feathers (239a), it is unlikely that the poet would return to a renewal of the flesh here. But the word in the poem for 'bird, young bird' is *brid* (235, 372) and Emerson's justification for his translation is not convincing. *Brǣd* is better translated 'flesh' ; it

is probably cognate with OHG *brāt, brāto*, 'tender, edible meat' and ON *bráð*, 'raw meat'; see A. Jóhannesson, *Isländisches Etymologisches Wörterbuch*, pp. 613-14. It is natural that the flesh which perished in the fire (221-2) should be restored. It is not valid to say that because the bird's feathers have already been discussed the poet would not return to the flesh, for the poet does not always follow a logical order. From the *synnum āsundrad* (242) it is clear that the poet had the allegorical interpretation in mind and that he was thinking of the resurrection of the flesh. Furthermore this passage in which the renewal of the flesh is mentioned introduces the simile of the rebirth of the seed, which also symbolises the resurrection of the flesh. At the end of the simile we hear again of the renewal of the bird and its flesh (257-9). So translate *brǣd* as 'flesh' here. The word may be related to *gebrēadad* (372) and *gebrēdade* (592).

242a. Of **synnum āsundrad** Cook says 'the appropriateness of this is not evident'. But the phrase looks forward to the allegorical interpretation. The fire in which the phoenix is immolated corresponds to the purgatorial fire of Doomsday in which men's bodies are purged of all sins, cf. lines 544-5. The new flesh will not be the old mortal, sinful flesh, but a flesh without sin ; see further note to line 544. There is constant reference to the allegorical interpretation in the first half of the poem.

242 ff. The fathers made frequent use of the topos of the rebirth of the seed, together with a reawakening of all plant life, as a symbol for the resurrection of man at Doomsday. The topos is based ultimately on I Corinthians xv, 35-8. As the phoenix is also used as a symbol for the resurrection of man, the inclusion of the rebirth of the seed is obviously appropriate here. The seed resembled the phoenix particularly in that it is said to die in order to bring forth a new plant. As the seed and the phoenix are both symbols of resurrection, they are often linked together in the fathers. Thus Clement of Rome, in whose works this juxtaposition is met with for the first time, deals with the rebirth of the seed and then immediately afterwards with the phoenix (*First Epistle to the Corinthians*, XXIV-XXV). His words are echoed by Tertullian (*De resurrectione* XII-XIII) and Cyril of Jerusalem (*Catechesis* XVIII, 6-8). The most interesting example is found in the *De cursu stellarum* XI-XII, of Gregory of Tours, for in his discussion of miracles, the second is said to be the rebirth of the seed and the third is the story of the phoenix as told by Lactantius. For the phrase **sumes onlīce swā** Krapp-Dobbie compare *ǣghwæs* (44, 312) and *ealles* (581). They translate *sumes* as 'somewhat'. The *swā* of line 243 is to be understood as correlative with that of line 257 ; translate : 'Somewhat in the same way as (243) . . . so (257)'. It is better therefore to start a new sentence with *sumes* (242). **Hī** (247) refers to 'men, mankind'.

243. For **wǣsmas** cf. eOE *wæstmas* ; see 'Language' C (iv).

247. **Wraðu** means 'support', though Krapp-Dobbie suggest an

extension in meaning to 'sustenance'. But 'support' gives good
sense here for the poet has the allegorical interpretation in mind.
Just as the corn which a man has stored away in the summer will
provide him with sustenance in the winter, so the good deeds which
a man performs on earth will be his support when he comes to face
God at Doomsday.

248. For **gefēon** cf. eOE *gefēan* ; see 'Language' A (ii).

251. The phrase **eorla ēadwelan** has been suspected of being
corrupt because of the sg.verb *sceal*. But *ēadwelan* can be accepted
as a late OE orthographic variant of *eadwela*; see 'Language' C (vi)
c. **Ālǣdan** is intransitive here ; cf. *ālǣde* (233). For the meaning
of **þurh**, 'marking the efficient cause or reason, through, in con-
sequence of etc.', see BT s.v. *þurh* A III (3). The sense of the
passage is 'In accordance with the corn's natural processes, man's
riches, which are previously sown as pure seed, shall be produced
from these fruits'. We reap in the next world what we have sown
in this. It should be remembered that the sun symbolises Christ,
who at Doomsday will call forth the pure to participate in the joys
of heaven. Thus the riches (*wæstmas*) are to be understood as both
material in the shape of food and spiritual in the form of eternal
salvation, cf. line 586, *Elene* 1316. The mingling of the allegorical
and literal levels has made the passage a little harsh. The same
thought is repeated at lines 255-7. For the simile of the seed cf.
I Corinthians xv, 35-8 and John xii, 24.

254. Thorpe and Gollancz take **līfes tācen** to be parallel to
*woruldgestrēon* ; Gollancz translates 'then the sun's gleam in spring-
tide awakeneth the signs of life, the world's great wealth'. But it
is better with Schlotterose and Cook to understand *līfes tācen* as
parallel to *sunnan glǣm*. The sun is a symbol of life ; cf. *torht tācen
Godes* (96).

258. **Ednīwe** can be taken as either an adv. or an adj., which can
in its turn be either nom. or dat. It is perhaps best to take it as
the nom. of the adj. here ; cf. lines 266, 370, etc.

259. There was a great deal of speculation among classical
authors as to what the phoenix ate. The earlier writers, e.g. Pliny,
*Natural History* X, ii, 4, say that it was not known to eat anything ;
but Ovid, who is the first classical author to mention the phoenix's
food, says that it fed on the 'gum of frankincense and the juices of
amomum' (*Metamorphoses* XV, 394). Claudian has that its food
was 'the sun's clear beam' and its drink 'the sea's rare spray'
(*Carmina Minora* XXVII, 14-16) ; whereas the *Carmen* describes
its food as *ambrosios rores* (111). The first element of *meledēawes*
probably means 'honey' ; cf. Gothic *miliþ*, OHG *mili-tou*, and see
OED s.v. *mildew*.

263. **Fyrngesetu**, 'ancient seat', is found only here in Old English.
The poet had the allegorical interpretation in mind — man regaining
his old home from which he had been expelled at the time of Adam
and Eve ; cf. *ealdcȳðþu* (435). The *fyrngesetu* are to be contrasted

with the *sorgfulran gesetu* (417), the home of Adam and Eve in this world after they had been expelled from paradise.

267. The **of grēote** is introduced by the poet in order to link more closely the death of the phoenix with the death of man. The poet is preparing for the allegorical interpretation where the resurrection of the phoenix corresponds to the resurrection of men from their graves. But it leads in this passage to a curious mixture of cremation and inhumation ; cf. *bān gebrosnad* (270). Translate 'out of the grave'. On this passage see Blake, 51 ff.

278. **Sunbeorht gesetu** is found here and at line 436 where it is parallel to *ealdcȳðþu*. In both cases the phrase refers to the phoenix's home or paradise, though Cook says that the *sunbeorht gesetu* 'is properly Heliopolis in Egypt', where the bird is said to deposit the ashes of its parents in many sources. All MSS of the *Carmen* have *Solis ad ortus* (121) and there is no indication in the *Carmen* that Heliopolis was mentioned at all. Possibly the English poet connected the *ortus* here with that mentioned in line 3 and so understood the *Solis ad ortus* to be the phoenix's home.

280. For **feþerhoma** cf. *Genesis*, lines 417, 670, *Solomon and Saturn*, line 151.

282. One can only assume from the **þǣr** that the phoenix buried the ashes of its parent in its own house after it had returned ; in the *Carmen* the phoenix left them on the altar at Heliopolis. But the phoenix's return journey is dealt with both here and at lines 320 ff. and the two accounts do not harmonise completely. In the first it implies the phoenix flew straight home from Syria to bury its parent. In the second the phoenix appears to fly round the world. Somewhere on this journey it is joined by the other birds who follow it to paradise.

285. **Ascan** should be read with *bān* : 'he brings the bones . . . the ashes as well'. The burial of the ashes is not a common feature in classical authors though it is found in Herodotus, *History* II, 73, and Achilles Tatius, *Clitophon and Leucippe* III, 25. In the *Carmen* the phoenix lays its ashes on the altar.

288. Thorpe and others read *segn* for the MS **þegn,** the phrase *þǣre sunnan segn* being translated 'the sign of the sun', which is the 'sun itself and all it signifies' (Emerson, p. 20 (n.)). Emerson justifies the emendation on the grounds that the poet omits all reference to the subservience of the phoenix to the sun. But this is to emend the text on the basis of a theory instead of basing the theory on the text. It is unlikely that the poet would refer to the renewal of the sun for the phoenix, for the whole emphasis of the text is on the renewal of the phoenix itself. The phrase *þǣre sunnan þegn* makes excellent sense if translated 'the servant of the sun', for despite Emerson the phoenix appears in this capacity in lines 90-147 ; see above note to line 90. The sun is used as a symbol for God in the Bible (Fitzpatrick p. 36), and in *The Phoenix* the sun is a symbol for Christ, cf. lines 587-8. The phoenix addresses his

song to the sun (124) just as the blessed address their praises to Christ (615-17). The phoenix 'serves' the sun in the same way as the blessed serve Christ. Cook suggested that the OE *þegn* was suggested by the Latin *satelles*.

291. Descriptions of the phoenix are common and occur as early as Herodotus, *History* II, 73. The commonly recurring features are the brilliant colours, the diadem, its resemblance to the eagle or the peacock and, particularly in Christian authors, its radiance.

294. For **wrixleð** cf. eOE *wrixled*, see 'Language' C (iii) a.

296b. Holthausen, *AB*, ix (1899), 356, and Schlotterose have questioned this half-line on metrical grounds, but editors have generally not emended. As Krapp-Dobbie rightly point out the *blācum* must echo the *fulvo metallo* of *Carmen* 131 and so must mean 'bright'; and Holthausen's suggestion of *blacum*, 'black', is not acceptable. Metrically the half-line can be interpreted as a hypermetrical Type a line which can have from one to eight preliminary unstressed syllables; see A. J. Bliss, *The Metre of Beowulf*, 1958, p. 94. This type, however, is generally confined to the *a*-verse, and Bliss lists only one example of a hypermetric line with one preliminary unstressed syllable : *mid synna fyrnum* (*The Order of the World* 102), though he thinks it probably corrupt.

301. *Gebyrd* generally means 'nature' (cf. line 360), and Cosijn, *Beitr.*, xxiii (1898), 122, has suggested that *gebyrd* is here used like *gecynde* (356). Krapp-Dobbie accept this and translate **ēaggebyrd** as 'the nature, or power, of the eye'. But Schlotterose (after Trautmann) claimed that it is the eye itself rather than the faculty of the eye which is likely to be compared with a precious stone set in gold. He emended to *ēaggebrygd* 'das funkeln der augen' and compared *blēobrygdum* (292). Other editors keep the MS reading which they translate as 'eye' or 'eyeball'. But it must be admitted that *ēaggebyrd* is more likely to mean 'eye's nature', and we can perhaps translate with Kennedy (p. 321) : 'The nature of its eye is stark, in hue most like to stone'.

305. Because of the inclusion of *swēoran* we must assume that the English poet thought the phoenix had brilliant plumage round its neck, cf. *auri fulgore circa colla* (Pliny, *Natural History* X, ii, 3). But the *Carmen* and most other descriptions of the phoenix give the bird a diadem, and the blessed are said to have crowns (or haloes) in the second half, lines 602-4.

308. The meaning of **scyld** is uncertain here, the *Carmen* having *hoc cervix summaque terga nitent* (130). BT s.v. *scild* III say it 'is used of a bird's back (as being shield-shaped ? or can *scyld* here be connected with *sculdor* ? cf. (?) *shield-bone* = shoulder-blade quoted by Halliwell. *Icel. skjöldr* is used of shield-shaped things)'. Bright glosses it as 'shield (portion of a bird's plumage)'. Emerson, p. 24, thinks it is the 'back as opposed to the belly' which is designed for giving protection. He compares the modern zoological sense of *shield* for the back of bird or beast, and the use in *Sir Gawain and*

*the Green Knight* for the back of the boar (1456, 1626). But the phoenix has no need of protection and the protected back does not harmonise with the rest of the description. I would suggest that *scyld* here refers to a crest on the head, which is characteristic of the peacock, a bird with which the phoenix is often compared. This crest is often of great beauty and is shaped like a shield ; cf. Pliny's phoenix with *caputque plumeo apice honestante* (Natural History X, ii, 3), and Solinus' with *capite honorato in conum plumis extantibus* (*Collectanea Rerum Memorabilium*, ed. Th. Mommsen, p. 149). Brunetto Latini in his *Li Livres dou tresor* (ed. F. J. Carmody, 1948, p. 147) makes use of this passage in Solinus, but he writes specifically of the phoenix *ele a creste*. Cf. the ON *rauð rǫnd*.

311. **Fōtas** for the more usual *fēt* ; cf. *tōpas* (407). The form *fōten* occurs in *PP*.

312. **Ǣnlīc** is used also of the phoenix's home (9). The interpretation 'unique' suggested by Thorpe is perhaps the best here ; cf. *spearuwan . . . ānlīcum fugele : sicut passer unicus* (Psalm ci, 5). The phoenix is likened to an eagle in the earliest authors, though in early Christian authors it is particularly compared with the peacock.

314-17. Although this passage is suggested by the *Carmen*, the English poet has coloured it with Christian implications. The blessed, like the phoenix, are eager for salvation through death and they are not slothful in their attempt to win salvation. They are also bright and shining. The wicked, on the other hand (i.e. the other birds), are slothful and lascivious. The word **hygegǣlsa** is a hapax legomenon ; but *hygegāla* (*Riddle* 12/12) means 'lascivious, wanton', and *gǣlsa* means 'luxury, extravagance', cf. *Juliana* 364-8 where the devil is ready to corrupt someone with *mōdes gǣlsan*, 'wantonness of spirit'. *Hygegǣlsa* is generally translated 'slow, sluggish', but in view of these parallels it is better to interpret it as 'wanton, lightminded' ; cf. Thorpe's translation 'nor in habit wanton'. The English poet has the allegorical interpretation in mind.

322. **Swā** here means 'when' ; cf. line 41. Krapp-Dobbie omit the comma after *oðēaweð* and imply a reading *mongum folcum monna*. But it is better to read *mongum monna* as parallel to *folcum*, cf. lines 4-5, 170.

327 ff. After its resurrection the phoenix reveals itself to all mankind. This passage corresponds to 508 ff., where after the resurrection of mankind at Doomsday the phoenix, symbolising Christ, is again made manifest to all men.

330. **Fǣgran** must be a comparative to bring it into line with *sellīcran* (329). Emendation to *fǣgerran* is unnecessary, see 'Language' B (ii). Cosijn, *Beitr.*, xxiii (1898), 123, compares the use of *ofer* after a comparative with *Orosius*, p. 34 : *glēawra ofer hī ealle*.

332. In view of the parallel of line 425 (cf. also lines 313, 655) it is unnecessary to emend **gewritu** to *gewritum*, as most editors have done since Grundtvig first suggested it. Gollancz does not

emend and translates : 'and their writings reveal it, with their hands they design it in marble-stone'. It is best to understand *ond gewritu cȳþað* in parenthesis and to take *weras* as the subject of *mearciað*.

336. For **on healfa gehwōre** see N. Blake, 'Two notes on the Exeter Book', *NQ*, ccvii (1962), 45-7.

352 ff. C. W. Kennedy, *The Earliest English Poetry*, 1943, p. 297, claimed that the grief of the birds as they are turned away from paradise was developed as an allegory of 'the sadness of the disciples who remained behind on earth' at Christ's Ascension. But there is nothing in the poem which supports this claim. In the poem the birds symbolise the blessed who follow Christ in heaven (591-4). It is difficult to know how to interpret this feature of the poem, but it is possible that there is a clue to its interpretation in the echo of *gēomormōde* at lines 411-13. Is it not possible that the sadness of the birds on leaving paradise is an allegory of the sadness of Adam and Eve when they were expelled from paradise after the fall ?

356. Bright and Hall translate **gecynde** as 'nature' ; others as 'sex'.

357. Many of the early classical authorities gave the bird's sex as male and Ovid is the first author to claim that the bird is female. But most late classical and Christian authors prefer to plead ignorance about the bird's sex ; see further Fitzpatrick, p. 21.

375. Thorpe and Gollancz translate **swǣs** as 'tender', but Schlotterose and Cook translate 'own' because of the *Carmen's suus (heres)*. *Swǣs* is commonly used with nouns of relationship in the sense of '(one's) own dear', cf. *swǣs fæder (Elene* 517) and *wið fæder swǣsne (Crist* 617) ; see BT s.v. *swǣs* II. Translate : 'he is to himself a son and his own dear father'.

377. Grundtvig suggested reading *meahtiga* for **meahta,** an emendation accepted by Ettmüller and Cook ; Schlotterose has *meahtga*. But Krapp-Dobbie rightly compare *meahtan dryhtnes (Crist* 868) and *meahte dōmas* (Psalm cxviii, 13).

382. The poet introduces the idea that man can win salvation only after he has gone through a period of suffering on earth. It is presumably this suffering which such people as the wanderer and the seafarer are experiencing on earth. The way of Christ had led through suffering to resurrection ; the Christian here on earth is expected to take part in the sufferings of Christ in order that he might afterwards share in His glory, cf. Romans viii, 17. The phoenix which symbolises both man and Christ unifies the concept.

386. Klæber, *JEGP*, vi (1906-7), 198, comparing line 475 suggested emending **in worulde** to *on wuldre*, though Hall had earlier (1902) proposed the translation 'in glory'. Cook and Krapp-Dobbie have *in wuldre* ; Gollancz retains the MS reading, translating 'dwell in that world'. This makes excellent sense and line 662 shows that *woruld* was not confined to this transitory world. Klæber's emendation is tempting, but there is not sufficient justification for departing from the MS here.

387. **Gelīces** is a partitive gen. and opens the allegory proper.
**In burgum** has the sense of 'on earth'.

396. Thorpe's emendation of **scēates** to *scēata* is accepted by
Ettmüller and all later editors. The phrase *foldan scēat* is normally
found only in the plural and here we would expect a plural dependent
upon the superlative *sēlestan*. But *foldan scēatas* means 'the quarters
of the world, i.e. the whole world', whereas the sg. *foldan scēat* refers
to one particular part of the world, i.e. paradise. So perhaps we
should retain the sg. here in this sense, a usage confined to the poet
of *The Phoenix*, even though the plural might be considered more
grammatically correct. Cf. *ēðles wyn* (411), for *wyn* in this poem
generally has a gen.pl. dependent on it.

402. The fall and redemption of man are closely linked with a
tree in the poem. It is because Adam and Eve tasted of the fruit
of the tree of knowledge of good and evil in paradise that they were
expelled. It is not too fanciful to think that it was upon this tree, the
highest in the garden, that the phoenix perched. Yet the fruit of
this tree (465 ff.) symbolises the good deeds by which man can
achieve salvation and thus re-entry into paradise.

404. It is possible to take **forbodene** as an orthographic variant
of *forbodenne* agreeing with *æppel*.

407. All scholars agree that it is extremely difficult to make any
sense out of lines 407-8 as they stand in the MS and that there has
probably been some corruption in the text. In line 407 the plural
form **tōþas** for *tēþ* arouses our suspicion, but its genuineness is
proved by *fōtas* (311), *tōþas* (*Soul and Body II* 114, Psalm lvii 5),
and by the alliteration which one would expect to fall on a noun.
The word *īdge* makes excellent sense if interpreted as the nom.pl.m.
of the adj. *īdig*, 'busy, active'. This interpretation was put forward
by F. Holthausen in his *Altenglisches Etymologisches Wörterbuch* s.v.
*īdig*, where it is compared with Swedish *idog* and ON *ið*. This
etymology has received the support of A. Jóhannesson, *Isländisches
Etymologisches Wörterbuch*, pp. 1-2, and J. de Vries, *Altnordisches
Etymologisches Wörterbuch* s.v. *ið* 1. Many other suggestions have
been made but few of them are of any value.

408. If the MS reading of line 407b is accepted, the assumed corruption of these lines must be located in line 408a, which in the MS
reads *āgeald æfter gylte*. But as the **æfter gylte**, 'on account of their
sin', makes perfect sense in the context, one is left with the answer
that if these lines contain a corruption, it must be in the MS
*āgeald*. The form is certainly suspicious, for one would have
expected a past participle dependent on *wurdon*. Grein-Köhler,
*Sprachschatz der angelsächsischen Dichter*, 1912, s.v. *āgylden*, take
*āgeald* as the pp. of *āgeldan*, 'punire'. But this is improbable as
*āgeald* is the form of the pret.sg. of this verb. Schlotterose and
Klæber accept Trautmann's emendation to *āgǣled*, though this
means to 'hinder, neglect, delay' and hardly seems appropriate
here. Brett, *Modern Language Review*, xxii (1927), 259-60, suggests

that *āgeald* could be a noun meaning 'a payment, recompense' or the 3 sg.pret. of *āgeldan*. Yet in order to accept either of these interpretations one must also accept Brett's suggestion that *idge* is a corrupt or late form of *ecge, icce* ; and even then the sense is not very comfortable. In order to restore that fluency of style so characteristic of the poem, I suggest emending *āgeald* to either *āgolden* or *āgold(e)ne*. The latter would be the more normal form, but the former is supported by the line *hælepa heolstorcofan onhliden weorpað* (49), the only other example where *weorpan* in a plural person is used with a pp. I have therefore adopted *āgolden*. How *āgolden* became *āgeald* is difficult to guess, but I suggest the following facts might be taken into consideration. Corruption of the stressed vowel occurs in such cases as *bregden* for *brogden* (306). The omission of *n* occurs frequently in the Exeter Book. If corruption had started along these lines, it is possible that a scribe 'corrected' what was in his copy to *āgeald*.

420 ff. This refers to Christ in His rôle as the second Adam, and thus He is fittingly contrasted with the first Adam.

424 ff. **Is þon gelīcast** (424) answers to *swā ðā foregengan* (437) ; see A. Campbell, 'The Old English Epic Style', *English and Medieval Studies* (1962), p. 20 (n.).

433. **Geong** is best taken as acc.sg.n. agreeing with *feorh*, 'renewed life, youth', though it is also possible to accept with Thorpe that it agrees with the phoenix : 'that, young, it spirit again may receive'. But Grundtvig and others read *feorhgeong* (*feorh-geong*). Yet the parallel of ll. 189-92 were *feorg geong* is contrasted with *þā yldu* and the fact that *feorhgeong* is not found elsewhere make *feorh geong* a better reading.

441-2. Adam and Eve, and thus all men, lost the protection which paradise gave on account of original sin and were therefore subject to the torments inflicted on them in this world by the devil. It is only when they re-win paradise that they escape again from the devil's persecution (447-50). It is unlikely that *hearmra, hettende* and *āglǣcan* refer to men, as Kennedy, p. 325, translates.

443 ff. This passage is based on Ambrose's *Hexameron* ; see 'Sources, Authorship and Date' and Appendix I(b).

450. Barnouw, *Textkritische Untersuchungen*, 1902, p. 201, suggested reading *þās* for *þā*, as the poet uses *þās* when the reference is to earthly time (cf. 139, 390) and *þā* when the reference is to Doomsday (cf. 509, 517). But Gaebler, *Anglia*, iii (1880), 518, has pointed out that the poet was using Ambrose's *Hexameron* here and that *on þā frēcnan tīd* corresponds to the Latin *in die malo* (Doomsday). Emendation is therefore unnecessary.

451 ff. That one should build a refuge in heaven by distributing riches among the poor is also found in Chrysostom's *Homiliæ XXI de statuis* II, 5 (*Pat. Gr.* XLIX, col. 41).

455-6. Ettmüller and Gollancz have no punctuation at the end of line 455 and Gollancz translates 'hasteneth forth from this frail life'. But it gives better sense in the context to put a comma after **ōnetteð** and to accept it in the intransitive sense of 'to be employed (well), to carry on (good) employment'; cf. *Crist* 1578-80, *Maxims I* 140 and OHG *an(n)azzan*, Gothic *anahaitan*.

477. For **eortan** cf. eOE *heortan*; see 'Language' C (i) b.

488. For **sendað** cf. eOE *sendeð*; see 'Language' B (i).

491. **Monge fȳra cynnes**, 'all mankind'; cf. lines 495-6. *Lǣded*, *lǣdad* and *lǣdde* have been proposed as emendations for **lǣdaþ**; but here *lǣdaþ* is an orthographic variant of *lǣded*; see 'Language' B (i), C (iii) a.

493. This is the only time in Old English that Doomsday is referred to as **seonoþ**. See further W. Deering, *The Anglo-Saxon Poets on the Judgment Day*, 1890, and A. Keiser, *The Influence of Christianity on the Vocabulary of Old English Poetry*, 1919, p. 123. Cf. *æt þām mæþle* (538).

499. The absence of death in paradise is frequently noted in the first half, cf. line 52.

506. The phrase **æpplede gold** is also found at *Juliana* 688 where it is parallel to *bēagas* and at *Elene* 1259 where it is parallel to *māðmas*. In both these cases they are gifts distributed in the banqueting hall. Despite the parallel of Old French *pomelé*, Modern French *pommelé*, 'made in the shape of an apple', the sense of *æpplede gold* can hardly be 'golden apples', for the idea of a golden apple-shaped object is completely alien to Anglo-Saxon, and indeed Germanic, archæology. *Æpplede* is more likely to refer to the colour or texture of the gold, gold being otherwise described as *rēad*, *beorht*, *scīr*, *smǣte*, etc., and a possible translation would seem to be 'dappled gold, gold with streaks in it'. Cf. Modern English *apple-green*, *apple-gray*, ON *apal-grár*.

508 ff. See note to lines 327 ff.

511. Cook reads *Anwalda* for **anwald** and this is accepted by Emerson, p. 28 (n.). But *anwald* in the sense 'power, divine power, potestas Dei', is quite suitable, for this is symbolised by the phoenix here, as at lines 646-7 : *fenix bēacnað . . . Godbearnes meaht*. For **āstellað** cf. eOE *āstelleð*; see 'Language' B (i).

512. Carleton Brown, *PMLA*, xviii (1903), 331-3, thought lines 512-17 were suggested by the *De trinitate* (*Pat. Lat.* XVII, col. 575). But this is unlikely ; see further 'Sources, Authorship and Date'.

513. **Lifes :** MS *liges*. For a similar confusion of *līf* and *līg* cf. *Fortunes of Men* 44. Thorpe and others keep the MS reading, and Emerson, p. 28 (n.), thinks that *liges gǣst*, 'spirit of fire', that is 'fire itself', is quite in keeping with the passage, for there is no fire in heaven and even Christ must summon fire for the work of destruction. In lines 519 ff. the souls are said to regain their bodies when the fire rises high to heaven. But it is doubtful whether *liges gǣst* can mean fire by itself and many editors have accepted Grundtvig's emendation to *līfes gǣst* in the sense 'the spirit of life' ; cf. *Guðlac* 838 : *leomu līc somud ond līfes gǣst*.

514-16. Christ shines on the blessed, as the sun on the phoenix. Cf. lines 117-18.

527. We should equate the **wræchwīl** with the *sārwracu* of line 382. After a period of suffering on earth a good man finds his reward in heaven at Doomsday ; cf. Lactantius, *The Divine Institutes* VII, v.

528. For **þæt . . . sind** cf. lines 13, 465, 655. The passage elaborates on lines 451 ff.

536-7. **His āgnum willum**, 'by his own choice, of his own accord' ; not as Kennedy, p. 328, translates, 'to his own gain'.

543. The verb **gewyrtian**, which is rare in Old English poetry, is especially used by the poet to link the allegorical interpretation with the story of the phoenix. The aromatic plants, *wyrta*, which the phoenix collects (193-6) are symbolical of the good works which devout Christians perform on earth (451-69) so that they may enter into the fire of purification without fear and emerge purified into paradise.

544. **Āmerian** occurs twice in *The Phoenix* (544, 633) and once in *Elene* where it refers to the purging of mortal sins by the fire of judgement :

> Hīe āsodene bēoð
> āsundrod fram synnum,  swā smǣte gold
> þæt in wylme bið  womma gehwylces
> þurh ofnes fȳr  eall geclǣnsod,
> āmered ond gemylted.  (1308-12)

As gold and silver are purified by burning the dross away, so is man cleansed of his sins. In most examples of the word in prose *āmerian* is also specifically used of that purification which is compared to the refining of precious metals. The thought is a common one in the Bible (cf. I Corinthians iii, 13-15) and the poet of *The Phoenix* no doubt had this conception in mind here. It will be noted that the verb *āsundrian* found in *Elene* 1309 is also used of the phoenix who rises *synnum āsundrad* (242). The phoenix, symbolising mankind, rises from the fire with a new covering of flesh which has been purged of all taint of sin. The sense of *clǣne* at lines 541 and 518 (*leahtra clǣne*) is therefore almost 'purified, cleansed', cf. *mānes āmerede* (633).

545. **Ābȳwan** is not found elsewhere in Old English, though *bȳwan* is used of polishing, possibly merely cleaning, of helmets at *Beowulf* 2257. The verb *bǣwenn* is also found several times in Orrm in such phrases as *to clennsenn and to bǣwenn hemm off alle þeʒʒre sinness* (18042-3). So *ābȳwan* means 'to clean, make pure'.

549. Job's testimony is also used in *Crist* 633 ff. The passage from Job is based on Job xxix, 18, though in the Vulgate this verse makes no mention of the phoenix. See further 'Sources, Authorship and Date' and G. Italie, 'De Phoenix', *Hermeneus*, xi (1939), 25-30. Job is introduced into the poem as the typical example of the suffering Christian on earth. He represents the good men of this

earth who despite their suffering (cf. *wræchwîl* 527) keep their faith in God and can look forward to future salvation. The phoenix also represents the blessed on earth and thus the phoenix and Job symbolise the same thing. It is fitting therefore that Job's song should echo the phoenix's ; note the verbal echo between lines 125-6 and 549-50. Just as the phoenix does not fear death (368-74), so Job and the good men in this world do not fear to die.

**553. Nêobed**—in *Genesis* 343 *nîobedd* is used of hell where it means something like 'bed of the dead', for *nêo-/nîo-* is cognate with Gothic *naus, nawis*, 'dead man', and ON *nár* 'corpse'. The element is also found in *orcnêas* (*Beowulf* 112). A similar concept to *nêobed* is found in the ON *nástrǫnd*. The passage in *The Phoenix*, which corresponds to the Vulgate *in nidulo meo moriar*, literally means 'I shall choose a bed of death in my nest'. *Nêobed cêosan* is thus almost a kenning for 'to die'.

**554.** For **hrâwêrig** cf. *wêrigmôd* (428).

**560b. Sêo dêore scolu** implicitly refers to the other birds grouped round the phoenix and singing praise to it ; cf. lines 344-5, 591-2.

**566.** Emerson, p. 29 (n.), thinks **âlŷseð** is 'pretty certainly chosen with relation to being released from the bondage of the grave, rather than redeemed in the spiritual sense. So *âweceð* "awake", as after a long sleep.' Cf. lines 489-90.

**574. Tâcen,** a common word in Old English religious writings, means 'a symbol' or 'a supernatural sign, a miracle', though both senses are applicable here. The bird symbolises the certainty of a future resurrection for man. There are several parallels between the cross as symbol (often in Old English poetry referred to as a *tâcen*) and the phoenix as symbol, both of which will reappear at the Day of Judgement. But the phoenix always remains a symbol ; it is never venerated in its own right.

**578.** By **Frêan geardas** the poet means paradise as both the home of the phoenix and the home of the blessed. It refers properly to the latter, but the poet has both the literal and allegorical meanings in mind (see note to lines 579-80). The phrase **sunnan tôgêanes** can be taken literally, i.e. to the east, or allegorically, the sun standing for Christ. The implication would seem to be that after resurrection at Doomsday the blessed take their old bodies to Christ in heaven just as the phoenix had taken its remains to paradise (276-9), although the allegorical interpretation in this particular form is not developed fully here or elsewhere in the poem.

**579-80.** The emendation of **hî wuniað** to *hê wunað* suggested by Thorpe is unnecessary, for the poet had both the literal and allegorical levels in mind here. The blessed, represented by the phoenix, assume their old bodies and go to heaven. There they live for ever (*fela wintra*) in bliss and security (lines 581-2 which refer back to lines 179-81 and cf. lines 594-5). One must assume that the bodies are at one and the same time the old bodies and yet miraculously rejuvenated and beautified.

586. The noble perfumes are the good deeds one performs on earth.

587. The sun is Christ, whom the blessed (the phoenix) serve. The allegory is carried on in line 589 where Christ is said to 'shine' on the souls.

590. In the sg. number **hrōf** is commonly used to describe the arch of the heavens which forms a roof for mankind, cf. *heofumhrōf* (173). But here the poet was possibly linking Christ with the sun, and thus Christ is said to shine high above the roofs (whether these be the housetops in this world or imaginary roofs in heaven).

591. A slight harshness is caused here by the shift in the allegory. In lines 587-8 Christ is represented allegorically by the sun, but at line 591 by the phoenix, who is followed by the other birds (i.e. the blessed). Previously the phoenix had stood for the blessed who worshipped Christ, the sun. See further 'The Form'.

592. **Gebrēdade** is probably related to *brēd*, see line 240 and note. The phrase **beorhte gebrēdade** would then mean 'with flesh beautifully restored, rejuvenated'. But because the poet changed his allegory at line 591 (see note), this has meant that the birds following the phoenix, who here stand for the blessed, are also by implication said to have undergone a resurrection of the flesh. This of course does not figure in the phoenix story in the first half. At line 594 the allegory shifts again and the blessed are once more represented by the phoenix.

598-9. Cook takes **weorc** as nom.sg. to agree with **blīceð** ; Schlotterose emends to *blīcað*. Tupper, *PMLA*, xxv (1910), 175, suggests that it is quite in accord with grammatical licence to have a neuter plural subject (*weorc*) followed by a sg. verb (*blīceð*), a suggestion also made by Thorpe. But it might be more satisfactory to assume that *blīceð* is an orthographic variant of *blīcað* ; see 'Language' B (i). It is of course also possible to take *weorc* as a sg. with Cook, though it is otherwise used only in the plural in the poem, cf. lines 386, 475, 527 and cf. next note.

598-601. The passage translates *Et omnia opera illorum velut sol in conspectu Dei* (Ecclesiasticus xvii, 16).

610. **Fǣgrum frǣtwum** are here 'good works', cf. lines 526-8.

611 ff. Cf. lines 50 ff. Similar passages occur in *Crist* 1660 ff., *The Judgement Day II*, 254 ff. and the ninth Vercelli Homily (M. Förster, *Der Vercelli-Codex CXVII*, 1913, pp. 96-7). These things absent from paradise are characteristic of man's turbulent and transitory life on earth.

613. For **hearde**, cf. eOE *hearda* ; see 'Language' B (i).

614. Christ is here portrayed in the rôle of a Germanic lord dealing out gifts to his retainers. Cf. *Crist* 1662-3. The retainers for their part praise the king, as the phoenix sang to the sun, cf. line 124.

622-4. Cook suggests that these lines are based on Revelation vii, 12.

624a. At *Guðlac* 1042 *gingra geafena* is used of heavenly gifts, but at *Gifts of Men* 2 *geongra geofona* is used of earthly gifts. The sense of *geong* here is not altogether clear, unless one assumes that the gifts are perpetually new. It is possible that the poet meant *geongra geofona* to echo *geong geofona ful* (267). One can take *geongra geofona* to be parallel to *gōda gehwylces* or to be dependent upon it. In view of the parallels quoted, the former is preferable.

625. One must understand a part of the verb 'to be'. For **strenðu** cf. eOE *strengðu* ; see 'Language' C (iv).

626 ff. Cook noted that these lines were based on the Sanctus and it is thus a fitting song for the righteous to sing.

635. For **singad** cf. eOE *singað* ; see 'Language' C (iii) b.

636. Most editors and translators open inverted commas here, which are closed at line 654, because of the *þæt sindon þā word* (655). But as the passage is addressed to God in the third person, as compared with lines 622-31, it is better to understand it as reported speech. Cf. such statements as *Soli sapienti Deo, per Jesum Christum, cui honor* etc. (Romans xvi, 27).

647. The **in geardum** here is to be equated with *tō Frēan geardum* (578). It is the phoenix's home, paradise and heaven.

648. The **hē** refers to the phoenix ; but the verb **onwæcned** would be more appropriate to describe Christ waking from death than the rebirth of the phoenix. For the form of **onwæcned** see 'Language' C (iii) b.

650. For **elpe** cf. eOE *helpe* ; see 'Language' C (i) b.

652 ff. In the Greek *Physiologus* we find 'The Phoenix resembles our Saviour who came from heaven with His two wings full of fragrance, that is, of virtuous celestial works, in order that we with holy prayers may extend our hands, and send up spiritual fragrance by means of our good lives'. (Quoted in Fitzpatrick, p. 26.)

654b. Kennedy, p. 332, translates 'and wingeth hence his flight' ; Gollancz has 'and is then impelled away'. But the sense of **āfȳsed** is 'to be eager (to do something)', cf. lines 274, 657. The meaning must be 'when the phoenix is eager (to get a new life)', he collects the precious scents. So Christ eager to save mankind had gone willingly to His death. Similarly those who long for salvation perform good deeds (i.e. collect precious spices) in order to achieve it, cf. lines 655 ff.

661-3. Cook compares Revelation i, 6 ; iv, 11, Jude 25. But it is common to conclude a work of this sort with praise to the Creator.

667. Short poetic texts made up of English in one and Latin in the other half-line are not infrequent. There is an interesting parallel in J. R. Lumby, *Be Domes Dæge*, 1876, p. 36. See also *Aldhelm* in *The Anglo-Saxon Minor Poems*, ed. E. v. K. Dobbie, 1942, pp. 97-8. The Latin words are glossed separately after the Old English Glossary.

668b. The form **merueri** is irregular, as it contains the ending of the passive infinitive attached to the stem of the preterite. Various emendations have been proposed. But most editors keep the MS reading, which seems preferable, because irregular forms occur frequently in medieval Latin words and it is not possible to apply the standards of classical Latin grammar. It means 'to get, obtain' ; see M. Bonnet, *Le Latin de Grégoire de Tours*, 1890, p. 606, n. 9.

670. For **mōtum,** see 'Language' C (vi) a.

671. Some editors and translators take **sēcan** with **maxima regna** and **gesittan** with **sedibus altis** ; cf. Kennedy, p. 332, 'that we may seek that mighty realm ; sit on high thrones'. But *gesittan* is best taken in the sense 'occupy', for *sēcan ond gesittan* is an alliterative phrase, cf. *Sume . . . sēcað ond gesittað . . . hāmas on heolstrum* (*Guðlac* 81-3). *Sedibus altis* is to be read with *lif an.*

673. The earliest editors keep **alma,** but Ettmüller and most later editors emend to *almæ* to agree with *letitiæ* (*letitię*). Schlotterose claims that a Latin adj. cannot agree with an Old English noun (despite the fact that *blandem et mittem* agree with *frēan*, lines 674-5), and that even if it should we would have expected the acc.pl.f. *almas* to agree with *eardinga*. The sense is better if we take *alma* to agree with *eardinga*. So one can either emend to *almas,* or leave the form assuming that either the poet's or the scribe's command of Latin was not perfect or that he was influenced by the OE acc.pl.f. in -*a* and wrote the form *alma* because of this. The influence of Old English orthography on Latin orthography is shown by the form *mittem* (674).

674. **Mittem** for *mitem,* acc. of *mitis.* It may be assumed that the common late Old English orthographic doubling of consonants has influenced the Latin form.

# APPENDIX I

## (a) *Carmen de ave phoenice*

THE following text is based on that in A. Riese's *Anthologia
Latina I* (1906), No. 485a, with one or two slight modifications.
For a complete list of variant readings reference should be
made to Riese, Fitzpatrick or Richmond.

Est locus in primo felix oriente remotus,
Qua patet aeterni maxima porta poli,
Nec tamen aestivos hiemisve propinquus ad ortus,
Sed qua sol verno fundit ab axe diem.
Illic planities tractus diffundit apertos,
Nec tumulus crescit nec cava vallis hiat ;
Sed nostros montes, quorum iuga celsa putantur,
Per bis sex ulnas imminet ille locus.
Hic Solis nemus est et consitus arbore multa
10 Lucus, perpetuae frondis honore virens.
Cum Phaethonteis flagrasset ab ignibus axis,
Ille locus flammis inviolatus erat,
Et cum diluvium mersisset fluctibus orbem,
Deucalioneas exsuperavit aquas.
Non huc exsangues morbi, non aegra senectus,
Nec mors crudelis nec metus asper adest;
Nec scelus infandum nec opum vesana cupido
Cernitur aut ardens caedis amore furor ;
Luctus acerbus abest et egestas obsita pannis
20 Et curae insomnes et violenta fames.
Non ibi tempestas nec vis furit horrida venti
Nec gelido terram rore pruina tegit,
Nulla super campos tendit sua vellera nubes,
Nec cadit ex alto turbidus umor aquae.
Sed fons in medio est, quem 'vivum' nomine dicunt,
Perspicuus, lenis, dulcibus uber aquis,
Qui semel erumpens per singula tempora mensum
Duodecies undis inrigat omne nemus.
Hic genus arboreum procero stipite surgens
30 Non lapsura solo mitia poma gerit.
Hoc nemus, hos lucos avis incolit unica Phoenix:
Vnica sed vivit morte refecta sua.

Paret et obsequitur Phoebo memoranda satelles:
Hoc Natura parens munus habere dedit.
Lutea cum primum surgens Aurora rubescit,
Cum primum rosea sidera luce fugat,
Ter quater illa pias inmergit corpus in undas,
Ter quater e vivo gurgite libat aquam.
Tollitur ac summo considit in arboris altae
40 Vertice, quae totum despicit una nemus,
Et conversa novos Phoebi nascentis ad ortus
Expectat radios et iubar exoriens.
Atque ubi Sol pepulit fulgentis limina portae
Et primi emicuit luminis aura levis,
Incipit illa sacri modulamina fundere cantus
Et mira lucem voce ciere novam,
Quam nec aëdoniae voces nec tibia possit
Musica Cirrhaeis adsimulare modis,
Sed neque olor moriens imitari posse putatur
50 Nec Cylleneae fila canora lyrae.
Postquam Phoebus equos in aperta effudit Olympi
Atque orbem totum protulit usque means,
Illa ter alarum repetito verbere plaudit
Igniferumque caput ter venerata silet.
Atque eadem celeres etiam discriminat horas
Innarrabilibus nocte dieque sonis,
Antistes luci nemorumque verenda sacerdos
Et sola arcanis conscia, Phoebe, tuis.
Quae postquam vitae iam mille peregerit annos
60 Ac si reddiderint tempora longa gravem,
Vt reparet lapsum spatiis vergentibus aevum,
Adsuetum nemoris dulce cubile fugit.
Cumque renascendi studio loca sancta reliquit,
Tunc petit hunc orbem, mors ubi regna tenet.
Dirigit in Syriam celeres longaeva volatus,
Phoenices nomen cui dedit ipsa vetus,
Secretosque petit deserta per avia lucos,
Sicubi per saltus silva remota latet.
Tum legit aërio sublimem vertice palmam,
70 Quae Graium phoenix ex ave nomen habet,
In quam nulla nocens animans prorepere possit,
Lubricus aut serpens aut avis ulla rapax.
Tum ventos claudit pendentibus Aeolus antris,
Ne violent flabris aëra purpureum

Neu concreta noto nubes per inania caeli
Submoveat radios solis et obsit avi.
Construit inde sibi seu nidum sive sepulchrum ;
Nam perit, ut vivat : se tamen ipsa creat.
Colligit hinc sucos et odores divite silva,
80  Quos legit Assyrius, quos opulentus Araps,
Quos aut Pygmaeae gentes aut India carpit
Aut molli generat terra Sabaea sinu.
Cinnamon hic auramque procul spirantis amomi
Congerit et mixto balsama cum folio :
Non casiae mites nec olentis vimen acanthi
Nec turis lacrimae guttaque pinguis abest.
His addit teneras nardi pubentis aristas
Et sociat myrrae vim, panacea, tuam.
Protinus instructo corpus mutabile nido
90  Vitalique toro membra vieta locat.
Ore dehinc sucos membris circumque supraque
Inicit, exequiis inmoritura suis.
Tunc inter varios animam commendat odores,
Depositi tanti nec timet illa fidem.
Interea corpus genitali morte peremptum
Aestuat, et flammam parturit ipse calor,
Aetherioque procul de lumine concipit ignem :
Flagrat, et ambustum solvitur in cineres.
Quos velut in massam, generans in morte, coactos
100  Conflat, et effectum seminis instar habet.
Hinc animal primum sine membris fertur oriri,
Sed fertur vermi lacteus esse color.
Crescit, et emenso sopitur tempore certo,
Seque ovi teretis colligit in speciem.
Inde reformatur qualis fuit ante figura,
Et Phoenix ruptis pullulat exuviis,
Ac velut agrestes, cum filo ad saxa tenentur,
Mutari tineae papilione solent.
Non illi cibus est nostro concessus in orbe,
110  Nec cuiquam inplumem pascere cura subest.
Ambrosios libat caelesti nectare rores,
Stellifero tenues qui cecidere polo.
Hos legit, his alitur mediis in odoribus ales,
Donec maturam proferat effigiem.
Ast ubi primaeva coepit florere iuventa,
Evolat, ad patrias iam reditura domus.

Ante tamen, proprio quidquid de corpore restat,
Ossaque vel cineres exuviasque suas
Vnguine balsameo myrraque et ture Sabaeo
120 Condit et in formam conglobat ore pio.
Quam pedibus gestans contendit Solis ad ortus
Inque ara residens ponit in aede sacra.
Mirandam sese praestat praebetque verendam :
Tantus avi decor est, tantus abundat honor.
Primo qui color est malis sub sidere Cancri,
Cortice quae croceo Punica grana tegunt ;
Qualis inest foliis, quae fert agreste papaver,
Cum pandit vestes Flora rubente solo :
Hoc humeri pectusque decens velamine fulget ;
130 Hoc caput, hoc cervix summaque terga nitent.
Caudaque porrigitur fulvo distincta metallo,
In cuius maculis purpura mixta rubet.
Alarum pennas insignit desuper iris,
Pingere ceu nubem desuper aura solet.
Albicat insignis mixto viridante zmaragdo
Et puro cornu gemmea cuspis hiat.
Ingentes oculi : credas geminos hyacinthos,
Quorum de medio lucida flamma micat.
Arquatur cuncto capiti radiata corona,
140 Phoebei referens verticis alta decus.
Crura tegunt squamae fulvo distincta metallo ;
Ast ungues roseo tinguit honore color.
Effigies inter pavonis mixta figuram
Cernitur et pictam Phasidis inter avem.
Magnitiem terris Arabum quae gignitur ales
Vix aequare potest, seu fera seu sit avis.
Non tamen est tarda ut volucres, quae corpore magno
Incessus pigros per grave pondus habent,
Sed levis ac velox, regali plena decore :
150 Talis in aspectu se tenet usque hominum.
Huc venit Aegyptus tanti ad miracula visus
Et raram volucrem turba salutat ovans.
Protinus exculpunt sacrato in marmore formam
Et titulo signant remque diemque novo.
Contrahit in coetum sese genus omne volantum,
Nec praedae memor est ulla nec ulla metus.
Alituum stipata choro volat illa per altum
Turbaque prosequitur munere laeta pio.

Sed postquam puri pervenit ad aetheris auras,
160 Mox redit : illa suis conditur inde locis.
O fortunatae sortis felixque volucrum,
Cui de se nasci praestitit ipse deus.
Femina seu sexu seu masculus est seu neutrum :
Felix, quae Veneris foedera nulla colit.
Mors illi Venus est, sola est in morte voluptas :
Vt possit nasci, appetit ante mori.
Ipsa sibi proles, suus est pater et suus heres,
Nutrix ipsa sui, semper alumna sibi.
Ipsa quidem, sed non eadem est, eademque nec ipsa est,
170 Aeternam vitam mortis adepta bono.

## (b) Ambrose's *Hexameron*, Bk. V, ch. 79-80

The following passage is taken from *Corpus Scriptorum Ecclesiasticorum Latinorum*, vol. XXXII, pars 1 (1896), pp. 197-8.

Phoenix quoque auis in locis Arabiae perhibetur degere atque eam usque ad annos quingentos longaeuam aetatem producere. quae cum sibi finem uitae adesse aduerterit, facit sibi thecam de ture et murra et ceteris odoribus, in quam impleto uitae suae tempore intrat et moritur. de cuius umore carnis uermis exsurgit paulatimque adolescit ac processu statuti temporis induit alarum remigia atque in superioris auis speciem formamque reparatur. doceat igitur haec auis uel exemplo sui resurrectionem credere, quae sine exemplo et sine rationis perceptione ipsa sibi insignia resurrectionis instaurat. et utique aues propter hominem sunt, non homo propter auem. sit igitur exemplo nobis quia auctor et creator auium sanctos suos in perpetuum perire non patitur, qui auem unicam perire non passus resurgentem eam sui semine uoluit propagari. quis igitur huic adnuntiat diem mortis, ut faciat sibi thecam et inpleat eam bonis odoribus atque ingrediatur in eam et moriatur illic, ubi odoribus gratis faetor funeris possit aboleri ? fac et tu, homo, tibi thecam : expolians te ueterem hominem cum actibus suis nouum indue. theca tua, uagina tua Christus est, qui te protegat et abscondat in die malo. uis scire quia theca protectionis est ? pharetra inquit mea protexi eum. theca ergo tua est fides ; imple eam bonis uirtutum tuarum odoribus, hoc est castitatis, misericordiae atque iustitiae et in ipsa penetralia fidei suaui factorum

praestantium odore redolentia totus ingredere. ea te amictum
fide exitus uitae huius inueniat, ut possint ossa tua pinguescere
et sint sicut hortus ebrius, cuius cito suscitantur uirentia.
cognosce ergo diem mortis tuae, sicut cognouit et Paulus, qui
ait : certamen bonum certaui, cursum consummaui, fidem
seruaui. reposita est mihi corona iustitiae. intrauit igitur thecam
suam quasi bonus phoenix, quam bono repleuit odore martyrii.

# APPENDIX II

## (a) *The Prose Phoenix*

*The Prose Phoenix* is a name I have chosen to give to an account of the phoenix found in two late Old English MSS : British Museum, Cotton Vespasian D. xiv, fol. 166a-168a (V), and Cambridge, Corpus Christi College 198, fol. 374b-377a (C). Both of the MSS are fully described in N. R. Ker's *Catalogue of Manuscripts containing Anglo-Saxon*, 1957, No. 48 and 209 ; V is also described by M. Förster, 'Der Inhalt der altenglischen Handschrift Vespasianus D xiv', *Englische Studien*, liv (1920), 64-5. Both texts were edited by F. Kluge,[1] and V has also been edited by R. Warner.[2] Though C is possibly the more original of the two texts, it contains more textual corruptions and is not such an intelligible text. Consequently I have chosen to edit V here, though a few variations from C are noted. Kluge edited the texts partly in verse, partly in prose, but Warner edited V entirely in prose, though no explanation was offered by either editor for the form chosen. I have decided to follow Warner in editing the text in prose, for it seems more probable that it was written in a kind of alliterative prose similar to that found in Ælfric's and Wulfstan's homilies than that it was written in both prose and verse.

Sanctus Johannes ʒeseh ofer gārseg swylc hit ān land wǣre. Þā ʒenam hine se ængel and ʒebrōhte hine tō neorxenewange. Neorxenewange nis nāðer ne on heofene ne on eorðe. Sēo bōc sæʒð þæt Noes flōd wæs fēowrtig fedmen hēh ofer þā hēgesta dūnen þe on middenearde synden ; and neorxenewang is fēowrtiʒ fedme hērre þone Noes flōd wæs. And hit hangeð betwōnen heofonen[3] and eorðen wunderlīce, swā hit se Eall-wealdend ʒescōp. And hit is eall efenlang and efenbrād. Nis þǣre nāðer ne dene ne dūne ; ne þǣre ne byð ne forst ne snāw ne hagel ne reign ; ac þǣr is fons uite, þæt is līfes welle. Þonne kalendas Januarii inn gāð þonne flōwð sēo welle swā fæʒere

---

[1] 'Zu altenglischen Dichtungen. 3. Zum Phönix', *Englische Studien*, viii (1885), 474-9.

[2] R. D.-N. Warner, *Early English Homilies*, EETS Original Series 152, 1917, pp. 146-8.

[3] heofonen : heofoñ *V* ; heofonan *C* ; heofone *Kluge, Warner*.

and swā smoltlīce and nā dēoppere þone mann mæiჳ ჳewǣten
his finger on forewarde ofer eall þæt land.  And swā ჳelīce
ǣlce mōnðe āne sīðe þonne se mōnð inn cumð sēo welle onginð
flōwen.  And þǣr is se fægere wudeholt þe is ჳenemmed
Radionsaltus.  Þǣr is ǣlc trēow swā riht swā bolt and swā
hēh þæt nān eorðlīc mann ne ჳeseh swā hēh, ne seggen ne cann
hwilces cynnes hēo synden.  Ne fealleð þǣr nǣfre lēaf of, ac
hēo byð singrēne, wlitiჳ and wynsum, welena unrīm.  Neorxenewange is upprihte on ēastewearde þisse wurlde.  Nis þǣr
ne hete ne hunger, ne þǣr niht nēfre ne byð, ac simble dæiჳ.
Sunne þǣr scīneð seofen sīðe brihtlȳcor þone on þissen earde.
Þǣr wuneð on Godes ængles unrīm mid þān hālgen sāwlen
oðð dōmes dæiჳ.  Þǣr wuneð on ān fugel fæჳer, fenix gehāten.
Hē is mycel and mǣre swā se Mihtiჳe hine ჳescōp.  Hē is hlāford
ofer eall fugelcynn.  Ǣlcere wuca āne sīðe se fæჳere fugel hine
baðeð on þǣre līfes welle ; and þonne flīhð se fugel and ჳesett
uppe þæt hēgeste trōw onჳean þǣre hāten sunne.  Þonne scīnð
hē swā sunnelēome and hē gliteneð swilc hē gyldene sēo.  His
feðeren synden ængles feðeren gelīce.  His brēost and bile
brihte scīneð fæჳere and fāge ; fēawe synden swylce.  Hwat,
his ēagene twā æðele synden swā clǣne swā cristal and swā
scīre swā sunelēome.  His fēt synden blōdrēade bēჳen and se
bile hwīt.  Hwæt, se fægre fugel flīhð of his earde, sē þe is
fæჳere fenix ჳehāten.  Þonne wuneð hē witodlīce on Egipte-
lande fīftēne wucan feste tōgædere.  Þonne cumeð him tō
swā swā tō [1] heora kinge fageninde swyðe eall þæt fugelcinn ;
and fæჳere ჳegrēteð ealle fenix, wrītiჳeð and singeð ealle ābūten
him, ǣlc on his wīsen.  Ealle hine heriჳeð.  Þonne ferð þæt folc
feorrene, swȳðe wāfiჳeð and wundrigeð, wylcumiჳeð fenix.
'Hāl bēo þū, fenix, fugele fæჳerest.  Feorren þū cōme.  Þū
glitenest swā rēad gold, ealra fugela king, fenix ჳehāten.'
Þonne wyreceð hēo of wexe and wrīteð fenix and mēteð hine
fæჳere þǣr se mādme stant.  Þonne fagenegeð þǣre fugeles
ealle fægere and fāge, feale tōgædere fealleð tō fōten, fenix
grēteð.  His stemne is swā briht swā bēme and his swēora
swylce smēte gold ; and his forebrēost fæჳere ჳehēowed swylce
marmelstān mǣres cinnes.[2]  And him ōn rēad hēow rudeð on
þān hrynge ; [3] goldfelle ჳelīc gliteneð fenix.  Þonne færð eft se

[1] swā swā tō : swā swā tō tō *V*.
[2] mǣres cinnes : mǣrescinnes *V* ; mǣres cinnes *Kluge* ; mǣre
scinnes *Warner* ; mǣrost cynnes *C*.
[3] hrynge : ricჳe *C*.

fugel fæʒere tō his earde emb fīftēne wucan and fugeles maniʒe
ealle him ābūten efne fērden ufene and nyðene and on ælce
healfe oððet hēo nēhiʒet neorxenewange. Þǣr inn ʒefærð
fenix fugele fæʒerest and eall ōðer fugelcinn tō heora earden
ʒewǣndeð. Nū sæiʒð hēr Sanctus Johannes sōðen worden :
swā se Wyrhte cann þæt ǣfre binnen ān þūsend wintren þynceð
fenix þæt hē forealdod sēo, ʒegadered tōgædere ofer eall
paradis þā dēorwurðe bōges and hēapeð tōsamne. And þurh
Godes mihte and þǣre sunnelēome se hēap byð onǣled. And
þonne fealleð fenix on middan þæt micele fȳr and wurð for-
bǣrned eall tō dūste. Þonne on þān þriddan dæʒe ārīseð se
fæʒere fugel fenix of dēaðe and byð eft edʒung and færð tō
þǣre līfes welle and baðað hine þǣrinne. And him wexeð on
feðeren swā fæʒere swā hēo ǣfre fæʒerest wǣren. Þuss hē
dēð ǣfre binne þūsend wintren : hē hine forbǣrnð and eft
edʒung upp ārīseð. And næfð hē nǣnne ʒemaca and nān
mann ne wāt hweðer hit is þe karlfugel þe cwēnefugel, būte
God āne. Þes hālge fugel is fenix gehāten, wlitiʒ and wynsum,
swā hine God ʒescōp. And þuss hē sceal drīgen Drihtenes
wille, sē þe is on heofone hēh and hāliʒ, ealra kinge King.
Crīst ūs ʒeneriʒe þæt wē on wynne wuniʒen mōte mid þān þe
leofeð and rīxeð ā būte ænde. Amen.

## (b) An Old Norse Version of *The Prose Phoenix*

It was noted by Larsen [1] in 1942 that there are two extant
ON versions of *The Prose Phoenix*. Both of these are included
in longer works of a historical or encyclopaedic nature. The
one in MS AM. 764 4⁰ fol. 1a forms part of the *Annála bœklingr*,
which is a short history of the world. This history is preceded
by a short geographical introduction which contains the account
of paradise and the phoenix. The MS dates from the fourteenth
century.[2] The second version, and the one that is printed here,
is found in MS AM. 194 8⁰ fol. 7a-8a. The MS, which dates
from the fifteenth century, is a small encyclopaedia, the first
part of which is largely devoted to an itinerary for the use of
pilgrims going to the Holy Land. The itinerary is preceded
by a short geographical description of the world in which is

---

[1] H. Larsen, 'Notes on the Phoenix', *JEGP*, xli (1942), 79-84.
[2] For further details of the MS see *Katalog over den Arnamagnæanske Håndskriftsamling*, udgivet af Kommissionen for det
Arnamagnæanske Legat, vol. ii, 1894, No. 1882.

included the account of paradise and the phoenix.[1] The two versions are very similar and are clearly related to each other. 764 does not, however, contain the account of the phoenix which is found in 194 under the heading *Hoc dicit Johannes apostolus de paradiso*. But it does otherwise contain a slightly fuller account of paradise than that found in 194. It is probable that the two versions have used a common source. Larsen[2] thought that the two versions were derived from an OE version closely related to the extant OE versions. But if we accept Förster's suggestion that *PP* was based on a Latin sermon or homily,[3] it could be suggested that the ON versions are based ultimately on this posited Latin sermon or homily. There is not sufficient correspondence between the vocabulary of *PP* and that of the ON versions to warrant the theory that the ON text is based on an OE original. It should be noted, for example, that where both OE MSS read *cristal*, both ON MSS have the Latinate form *kristallus*.

## Hoc dicit Moyses de Paradiso

Paradisus heitir staðr sá er eigi á himnum ok eigi á jǫrðu, heldr er hann í miðju lopti iafnnær himni ok jǫrðu svá sem hon var sett af Guði. Paradisus er fjórir tigir mílna hærri en Nóa flóð varð. Paradisus er ǫll jafnlǫng ok jafnbreið. Þar er hvárki fjall né dalr ; þar er eigi frost né snjórr ; þar eru allir landskostir ; en þar er ekki íllkvikendi ok engi andmarki. Þar er brunnr góðr, sá heitir lífsbrunnr. Þar er einn fagr skógr ok dásamligr er heitir Radion saltus ; hann fǫlnar aldri. Þar er hvert tré rétt sem kolfr ok svá hátt at eigi má yfir sjá. Þar eru hvers kyns tré, þau er með allri fegrð standa ok bera á sér alls kyns blóm ok birti epla ok aldina með mǫrgu móti. Þar fellr aldri lauf af viði. Sjá skógr er í miðri Paradiso. Eitt

---

[1] For further details of the MS see *Katalog over den Arnamagnæanske Håndskriftsamling*, vol. ii, 1894, No. 2407, and the introduction of Kr. Kålund's *Alfræði Íslenzk. Islandsk encyklopædisk Litteratur. 1. Cod. Mbr. AM. 194, 8vo*, 1908. The latter contains a diplomatic edition of the MS ; for the passage on the phoenix see pp. 3-6. The account of the phoenix in this MS has also been printed by K. Gislason, *Prøver af oldnordisk Sprog og Literatur*, 1860, §xiii *Paradisus*, pp. 407-9.

[2] *Op. cit.*

[3] M. Förster, 'Der Inhalt der altenglischen Handschrift Vespasianus D xiv', *Englische Studien*, liv (1920), 64-5.

tré með ávexti var bannat Adami,[1] þar er í folgin vitra góðs ok ílls. Þar er hvárki hatr né hungr ; ok aldri er þar nótt né myrkr, heldr er hinn sami dagr ávalt ok skínn sól þar sjau hlutum bjartari en í þessum heim,[2] því at þar kømr við ǫll birti himintungla. Þar eru settir englar at reysta til skemtanar. Þangat skulu fara sálur góðra manna ok una þar til dómadags síðan er Guð lauk upp, þá er hann leiddi þangat ǫnd þjófs þess er líf sitt lét á krossinum. Í Paradiso er einn fugl er fenix heitir ; hann er harðla mikill ok undarligr at skepnu svá sem Guð skóp hann. Ok er hann dróttinn yfir ǫllum fuglum. Hann laugar sik í lífsbrunni ok flýgr upp á þat tré er hæst er í Paradiso í gegn sólu. Þá skínn af honum sem af sólargeisla : hann glóar allr sem gull. Fjaðrar hans eru líkari englum Guðs ; brjóst hans er svá fagrt ok nef sem áðr var sagt of fjaðrar. Augu hans eru sem kristallus ; fœtr hans eru sem blóð. En þá er sá inn fagri fenix flýgr upp ór Paradiso á Egiptaland ok er þar fimtán vikur, þá safnask til hans alls kyns fuglar ok syngja um hann á hverja lund. Þá heyra menn þat þeir er þar eru ok fara til hans hvaðan æfa ok mæla svá : 'Kom heill, Fenix, hingat til lands ; þú glóar allr sem gull rautt. Allra fugla ertu konungr.' Þá landsmenn gǫra[3] ór vaxi ok eiri annan fenix ok marka sem líkast at ǫllu. Allir fuglar falla til fóta honum ok tigna hann með glaðri rǫddu. Rauð rǫnd liggr eptir baki honum endilǫngu, fǫgr sem gull sé brent. Þá er fimtán vikur eru liðnar ferr inn fagri fenix aptr til Paradísar. Allir fuglar fljúga með honum sumir fyrir neðan hann en sumir fyrir ofan ok á hváratveggju hlið. En þá er þeir mega eigi fara lengra, þá ferr hverr til síns heima.

*Hoc dicit Johannes apostolus de Paradiso*

Þat var fjórum þúsundum vetra fyrir burð Krists, þá var ein þúsund gengin, þá var fenix gamall orðinn ok þá safnar hann sér fuglaliði miklu at bera saman viðkǫst mikinn. En af Guðs vilja varð svá þá er sól skein á viðkǫstinn ok af hita sólarinnar kom eldr í viðkǫstinn. En fenix féll ofan í eldinn miðjan ok brann allr at ǫsku. En eptir á hinum þriðja degi þá

---

[1] Adami : Adái *194* ; Adam *Gislason* ; Adami *Kálund*.
[2] heim : heï *194* ; heimi *Gislason* ; heim *Kálund*.
[3] gǫra (*MS* giera) : *written above line between* menn *and* ór *in a later hand* ; þa giera landz-menn *Kálund* ; þarlandsmenn gjöra *Gislason* ; ok er landsmenn heyra . . . þeir gǫra *764*.

reis hann upp af dauða ok er hann þá ungr í annat sinn ok ferr þá til lífsbrunns ok laugar sik þar. Þá vaxa honum fjaðrar sem þá er fegrstar váru. Hann verðr gamall um þúsund vetra, þá brennir hann sik í annat sinn ok rís upp ungr. En engi maðr veit hvárt hann er karlfugl eða kvennfugl nema Guð einn.

# GLOSSARIES

## OLD ENGLISH

THE Old English Glossary is intended to list all occurrences of words except adverbs, conjunctions, prepositions and pronouns. The order of the words is strictly alphabetical; æ follows **ad**; words prefixed by **ge-** follow **gearwian**; ð and þ are treated as one letter and follow **t**; whether the headword has ð or þ depends upon the form of the first reference which follows. The gender of nouns is indicated by the abbreviations *m.*, *f.*, *n.* (noun is implied). The numbers after *sv.* and *wv.* refer to the classes of strong and weak verbs respectively. The line references to emended forms are italicised. The glossary is intended to be used with the notes, which supplement it. Cross-references are normally given only in the case of irregular or variant spellings.

ā *adv.* ever, always 35, 180, 385, 596 ; *see* ō.

ābȳwan *wv.* 1 to clean, make pure 545.

ac *conj.* but 5, 19, 26 etc.

ācennan *wv.* 1 to bear, bring forth, produce 241, 256.

ācōlian *wv.* 2 to grow chill 228.

ād *m.* pyre, fire 230, 272, 365, 503.

ādlēg *m.* flame of the pyre 222.

ǣ *f.* law 457.

æfēst *n.* malice, hatred 401.

ǣfre *adv.* always, ever 40, 83, 128, 562, 608, 637.

æfter *prep. w. dat.* after (in time) 111, 223, 225 etc. ; after (in space) 343 ; according to, on account of 258, 408 ; æfter þon afterwards 238.

ǣg *n.* egg, *dat. pl.* ǣgerum 233.

ǣghwæs *adv.* in every respect, entirely 44, 312.

ǣghwylc *pron.* each, everyone 164.

ǣhtgestrēon *n.* riches, possessions 506.

ǣlan *wv.* 1 to burn, consume 222, 526.

ælde *mpl.* men 198, 509, 546.

ǣled *m.* fire, conflagration 522.

ǣledfȳr *n.* fire, conflagration 366.

ælmesse *f.* alms 453.

ælmihtig *adj.* almighty 356, 473, 627, 630 ; *wk. nom. sg. m.* Ælmihtiga The Almighty 393.

ǣnig *pron.* any 31, 59, 138, 357, 546, 581, *gen. sg. m.* ǣnges in any way 136.

ǣnlīc *adj.* unique, noble 9, 312, 536.

æppel *m.* apple 230, 403.

æpplede *adj.*, *acc. sg. n.* æpplede gold dappled gold, gold with streaks in it 506.

ǣr *adv.* before, formerly, soon 252, 268, 283 ; ǣr þon formerly 379.

ǣr *prep. w. dat.* before 107, 245.

ǣrdagas *mpl.* former days 414.

ǣrest *adv.* at first, first 235, 281.

ǣrist *f.* resurrection 495, 559, 572.

ǣrþon *conj.* before 40, 83.

ǣspring *n.* spring, fountain 104.

æt *prep. w. dat.* by, near, 104 ; at 110, 262, 477 ; in 239, 280, 328, 538.

ǣt *m. f.* food, repast 401, 405.

ætsomne *adv.* together 272.

æþele *adj.* noble, excellent 9, 20, 26, 43, 104, 164, 281, 346, 460, 500, 528, 586, 614 ; *superl.* 2, 93, 207, 431.

æþeling *m.* noble one, prince, Christ 319, 354.

æþelstenc *m.* sweet odour 195.

æþeltungol *m.* noble star 290.

āfēdan *wv.* 1 to support, sustain 263.

āflēon *sv.* 2 to leave, depart from 155.

āfyrran *wv.* 1 to remove 5.

āfȳsan *wv.* 1 to be eager 274, 654, 657.

āgan *v.* to have, possess 559, 673.

āgeldan *sv.* 3 to punish, *pp.* agolden *408.*

āgen *adj.* own 256, 264, 275, 528, 536.

āglǣca *m.* devil, evil being 442.

āhebban *sv.* 6 to lift up, raise 540.

āhȳdan *wv.* 1 to hide, conceal 96.

ālǣdan *wv.* 1 to be led forth 233, 251.

ālȳfan *wv.* 1 to grant, permit 667.

ālȳsan *wv.* 1 to loose, release 566.

āmerian *wv.* 1 to purify, cleanse 544, 633.

ān *num. adj.* one, alone 177, 355, 358, 487, 503, 522, 534, 598, 636.

ānforlǣtan *sv.* 7 to give up, renounce 438.

ānga *wk. adj.* only, sole 423.

ānhaga *m.* unique being 87 ; ānhoga 346.

ānhoga *see* ānhaga.

anwald *m.* power, divine power 511 ; *see* onwald.

ār *f.* honour 663.

āscæcan *sv.* 6 to shake, clap 144.

asce *f.* ashes 231, 285, 373, 576, 648.

āstellan *wv.* 1 to raise up, 3 *sg. pres.* āstellað 511.

āsundrian *wv.* 2 to separate, free 242.

āswebban *wv.* 1 to still, calm 186.

ātor *n.* poison, venom 449.

āweaxan *sv.* 7 to grow 265.

āweccan *wv.* 1 to awake 367, 567.

āwyrdan *wv.* 1 to destroy, spoil 247.


bæc *n.* back 309.

bǣl *n.* fire, pyre 47, 216, 227, 284.

bǣlþracu *f.* violence of fire 270.

bæð *n.* bath, immersion 110.

bān *n.* bone 221, 270, 271, 283, 286, 512, 575.

bānfæt *n.* body 229, 520.

basu *adj.* purple, crimson 296.

bēacen *n.* sign 107.

bēacnian *wv.* 2 to betoken, signify 389, 575, 646.

beaducræftig *adj.* valiant, brave 286.

bēag *m.* plumage round the throat 306 ; crown, halo 602.

beald *adj.* steadfast, bold 458, 550.

bealosorg *f.* baleful sorrow, anguish 409.

bēam *m.* tree 35, 112, 122, 171, 177, 202, 402, 447.

bearn *n.* child, son 396.

bearo *m.* forest, grove 67, 71, 80, 122, 148, 432.

bebyrgan *wv.* 1 to bury 286.

begietan *sv.* 5 to obtain, attain 669.

behealdan *see* bihealdan.

bēodan *sv.* 2 to proclaim 497.

beorg *m.* hill, mountain 21, 31.

beorgan *sv.* 3 to taste 110.

beorhstede *m.* mound, funeral pile 284.

**beorht** *adj.* light, glorious, bright 35, 122, 240, 389, 602 ; *superl.* 80, 227, 306 ; clear 128.

**beorhte** *adv.* brightly, splendidly 31, 545, 592, 599 ; *superl.* 179.

**beran** *sv.* 4 to carry, bear, 3 *sg. pres.* **biereð** 199.

**besettan** *wv.* 1 to surround, enclose 304, 530 ; to cover 297.

**beteldan** *see* **biteldan**.

**bewitigan** *wv.* 2 to watch 92.

**bī** *prep. w. dat.* in comparison with, concerning, about 388 ; *w. instr.* upon, by means of 262.

**bibaþian** *wv.* 2 to bathe 107.

**bibēodan** *sv.* 2 to bid, command 36.

**biclyppan** *wv.* 1 to seize, grasp 277.

**bīdan** *sv.* 1 to abide, remain 47.

**bidēglian** *wv.* 2 to conceal 98.

**biereð** *see* **beran**.

**bifōn** *sv.* 7 to invest, clothe 259, 380, 527, 535.

**bīgan** *wv.* 1 to bow, bend 459.

**bīgenga** *m.* inhabitant, *dat. sg.* **bīgenga** 148.

**bihealdan** *sv.* 7 to inhabit 87 ; to behold 90, 114.

**bihelan** *sv.* 4 to hide, conceal 170.

**bihȳdan** *wv.* 1 to conceal 170, 418.

**biniman** *sv.* 4 to bereave, deprive 488.

**bisettan** *see* **besettan**.

**bisorgian** *wv.* 2 to dread, fear 368.

**biswīcan** *sv.* 1 to deceive, beguile 413.

**biteldan** *sv.* 3 to cover, adorn, array 273, 555, 609 ; to surround 339.

**bitter** *adj.* harmful, noxious 179 ; bitter, grievous 404, 409.

**bitȳnan** *wv.* 1 to close 419.

**biþeccan** *wv.* 1 to cover 490, 605.

**biþringan** *sv.* 3 to encircle, surround 341.

**biweaxan** *sv.* 7 to overgrow, cover 310.

**biwindan** *sv.* 3 to invest, clothe 666.

**blāc** *adj.* bright, shining, white 296.

**blǣd** *m.* bliss 391 ; inspiration 549 ; fulness 662.

**blǣddæg** *m.* day of bliss 674.

**blǣst** *m.* blaze, flame 15, 434.

**blēd** *f.* fruit 35, 38, 71, 207, 402, 466.

**blēobrygd** *m.n.* variety of colours, variegated colour 292.

**blētsian** *sv.* 2 to bless, adore 620.

**blīcan** *sv.* 1 to shine 95, 115, 186, 599.

**bliss** *f.* joy 126, 592.

**blīþe** *adj.* joyous, glad 620 ; *wk. dat. sg. m.* **blīþam** 599.

**blōstma** *m.* blossom, flower 21, 74.

**brǣd** *f.* flesh 240.

**breahtm** *m.* sound, music 134.

**brecan** *sv.* 4 to burst forth, break 67 ; to destroy 504.

**bregdan** *sv.* 3 to furnish, set, inlay, *pp.* **brogden** *306*, 602.

**brego** *m.* lord, prince 497, 568 ; **bregu** 620.

**bregu** *see* **brego**.

**brēost** *n.* breast 292 ; mind, heart 458, 550, 568.

**brēostsefa** *m.* heart, spirit 126.

**brid** *m.* young bird, nestling 235, 372.

**brimcald** *adj.* cold as the sea 67, 110.

**bringan** *sv.* 3 to bring 660.

**brond** *m.* fire 216, 283.

**brosnian** *wv.* 2 to wither 38.

**brūcan** *sv.* 2 *w. gen.* to use, enjoy 148, 674.

**brūn** *adj.* brown, dusky 296.

**bryne** *m.* flame, fire, conflagration 229, 520, 545, 575.

**bū** *num.* both 402.

**būgan** *wv.* 1 to live, dwell 157.

burg *f.* city 475, 588, 633, 666 ;
  **in burgum** on earth 389.
burna *m.* spring, brook, fountain
  107.
būtan *prep. w. dat.* without 637,
  651.
būtan *conj.* unless, except 358.
bȳme *f.* trumpet 134, 497.
byre *m.* child, offspring 128, 409.
byrgan *wv.* 1 to taste, eat, 404.
byrgen *f.* grave, tomb, *dat. pl.*
  **byrgenum** 512.
byrnan *sv.* 3 to burn 214, 218,
  502, 531.

cald *adj.* chill, cold 59.
Cāsere *m.* emperor, God 634.
cempa *m.* soldier, champion 452,
  471.
cennan *wv.* 1 to bear, beget 639.
cēosan *sv.* 2 to choose 479, 553.
cild *n.* child 639.
clā *f.* talon 277.
clǣne *adj.* pure, purified,
  cleansed 167, 252, 459, 518,
  541.
clǣne *adv.* entirely, wholly 226.
clēowen *n.* ball, *dat. sg.* **clēowenne** 226.
cnēo *n.* knee 459, 514.
cnyssan *wv.* 1 to smite, afflict 59.
condel *f.* candle 91.
corn *n.* corn, grain of corn 252.
corðer *n.* band, multitude 167.
cræft *m.* knowledge, skill 344.
Crīst *m.* Christ 388, 514, 590.
cuman *sv.* 4 to come, go, return
  91, 93, 102, 222, 366, 484, 508.
cwealm *m.* agony 642.
cylegicel *m.* icicle 59.
cyme *m.* coming, advent 47, 53,
  107, 245, 490.
cyn *see* cynn.
cynegold *n.* diadem 605.
cyneþrym *m.* royal majesty 634.
cyning *m.* king 175, 344, 356,
  496, 514, 541, 614, 664.

cynn *n.* kind, race, lineage,
  species 159, 198, 335, 358, 492,
  535, 546 ; **cyn** 330.
cyrran *wv.* 1 to return 352.
cȳþan *wv.* 1 to make known,
  proclaim 30, 332, 344, 425,
  634.
cȳþþu *f.* home, native land 277.

dǣd *f.* deed, act, work 445, 452,
  463, 528.
dæg *m.* day 147, 334, 478, 644.
dægrēd *n.* dawn 98.
dæl *n.* dale 24.
dǣl *m.* part, portion 261.
dǣlan *wv.* 1 to distribute, bestow 453.
deal *adj.* proud 266.
dēað *m.* death 52, 88, 368, 383,
  434, 485, 499, 557, 583, 642.
dēaðdenu *f.* valley of death 416.
dēaðrǣced *n.* grave 48.
dēman *wv.* 1 to judge 494.
denu *f.* glen 24.
deorc *adj.* black 98, 383, 499.
dēore *adj.* dear, beloved 560.
dēormōd *adj.* brave, dauntless 88.
dōgorrīm *n.* number of days, time
  485.
dohtor *f.* daughter 406.
dōm *m.* judgement 48, 524 ;
  glory 642.
dōmlīc *adj.* glorious 445, 452.
drēam *m.* melody, sound 138 ;
  bliss, joy 482, 560, 658.
drēogan *sv.* 2 to fulfil 210.
drēosan *sv.* 2 to fall 34, 261.
drohtað *m.* abode, dwelling place
  88, 416.
drūsende *adj.* drooping 368.
dryht *f.* multitude, men 334.
dryhten *m.* lord, God 48, 138, 383,
  445, 452, 454, 463, 478, 494, 499,
  557, 560, 583, 597, 600, 658.
drȳmende *adj.* rejoicing, exult-
  ing 348.
dryre *m.* fall 16.

**duguð** *f.* host, throng 348, 494 ; provision, wealth, **dugeþa** 454.

**dūnscræf** *n.* ravine 24.

**duru** *f.* door 12.

**dwǣscan** *wv.* 1 to blot out, extinguish 456.

**ēac** *adv.* also 375.

**ēaca** *m.*, **tō ēacan** *adv.* besides, likewise 285.

**ēad** *n.* bliss, happiness 319, 398, 638.

**ēadig** *adj.* blessed, happy, righteous, upright 11, 279, 361, 381, 473, 482, 500, 526, 603, 621, 677 ; blessed, unscathed 20, 46.

**ēadwela** *m.* blessedness 586 ; *nom. sg.* **ēadwelan** 251.

**eafera** *m.* child, son 405.

**ēaggebyrd** *f.* nature of the eye 301.

**eal** *adj. see* **eall**.

**eal** *adv.* wholly, entirely 241, 285, 505.

**eald** *adj.* old, ancient 238, 321, 376.

**ealdcȳðþu** *f.* old home, former abode 351, 435.

**ealdfēond** *m.* old enemy, devil 401, 449.

**ealdor** *n.* life 487 ; **tō ealdre** for ever 40, 83, 562, 594.

**ealdordōm** *m.* sovereignty, dominion 158.

**eall** *adj.* all, the whole of 7, 42, 67, 77, 132, 177, 279, 495, 576, 628 ; **eal** 511.

**ealles** *adv.* altogether, wholly 581.

**ēalond** *n.* island 287.

**eard** *m.* home 87, 264, 275, 321, 346, 361, 427; earth, land 158, 354.

**earding** *f.* home, abode 673.

**eardstede** *m.* dwelling place 195.

**eardwīc** *n.* dwelling, house 431.

**earm** *adj.* hostile, wicked 442 ; poor 453.

**earn** *m.* eagle 235, 238.

**earnian** *wv.* 2 *w. gen.* to earn, win 484.

**ēastan** *adv.* from the east 102, 290, 325 ; **ēstan** 94.

**ēastdǣl** *m.* eastern part 2.

**ēastweg** *m.* eastern way 113.

**ēce** *adj.* eternal, everlasting 319, 381, 398, 411, 473, 482, 572, 600, 608, 636.

**ēce** *adv.* for ever 594.

**edgeong** *adj.* rejuvenated 373, 435, 536, 608 ; **edgiong** 581.

**edgiong** *see* **edgeong**.

**ednīwe** *adj.* renewed, restored 77, 223, 241, 258, 287, 370, 558.

**ednīwinga** *adv.* anew, once more 534.

**edwenden** *f.* change, end 40.

**efenhlēoþor** *m.* concord of voices, united voice 621.

**eft** *adv.* afterwards, in due season, again, once more 222, 224, 231, etc.

**egeslīc** *adj.* dreadful, terrible 522.

**egsa** *m.* fear, terror 461.

**ellen** *m.n.* strength, courage 484.

**elp** *f.* help, succour 650.

**ende** *m.* end 365, 484, 562, 637, 651.

**endian** *wv.* 2 to end, bring to an end 83.

**enge** *adj.* narrow 52.

**engel** *m.* angel 492, 497, 568, 610, 621, 629, 677.

**eorcnanstān** *m.* precious stone 603.

**ēoredciest** *f.* crowd, troop of cavalry 325.

**eorl** *m.* man, warrior 251, 482.

**eorte** *see* **heorte**.

**eorþe** *f.* earth 43, 131, 136, 154, 207, 243, 249, 331, 349, 460, 487, 506, 629, 638.

**eorðweg** *m.* earth 178.

**ēst** *f.* grace, will 46, 403.

**ēstan** *see* **ēastan**.

**ēþel** *m.* earth, land 158, 392 ; home, native land 349, 411, 427.

**ēþellond** *n.* native land, home, 279.

**ēþelturf** *f.* earth, land 321.

**fācen** *n.* guile, evil 450, 595.

**fǣcne** *adj.* guileful, malicious 415.

**fæder** *m.* father 95, 197, 375, 390, 455, 492, 610, 627, 630, 646.

**fǣge** *adj.* doomed to death 221.

**fæger** *adj.* fair, beautiful 64, 85, 125, 182, 232, 236, 291, 307, 328, 352, 360, 510, 610, 654 ; *comp. acc. pl. f.* **fægran** 330 ; sweet, pleasant, *superl.* 8.

**fægre** *adv.* beautifully, gloriously 274, 295, 585, 627.

**fǣringa** *adv.* suddenly 531.

**fæst** *adj.* fast, firm, secure 172, 468.

**fæste** *adv.* firmly, securely 419, 569.

**fæðm** *m.* depth, bosom 487, 556.

**fæðmrīm** *n.* cubit 29.

**fāg** *adj.* variegated, adorned 292.

**fāh** *adj.* hostile 595.

**faran** *sv.* 6 to go, journey 123, 326.

**feallan** *sv.* 7 to fall 61, 74.

**fealo** *adj.* pale, yellow, fallow 74, 218, 311.

**fela** *adj. indecl. w. gen.* much, many 387, 580.

**feld** *m.* field, plain 26.

**feng** *m.* grasp, grip 215.

**fenix** *m.* phoenix (bird) 86, 218, 340, 558, 597, 646 ; phoenix (palmtree) 174.

**fēond** *m.* enemy, devil 419, 595.

**feor** *adv.* far 1, 192, 415.

**feorg** *see* **feorh.**

**feorh** *m.n.* life, body 223, 263, 266, 280, 371, 433, 558 ; **feorg** 192.

**feorhhord** *n.* soul, spirit 221.

P.—H 2

**feormian** *wv.* 2 to consume 218.

**feorran** *adv.* from afar 326.

**ferð** *m.n.* mind, soul, heart 415 ; **ferþþe** 504.

**feþer** *f.* wing, feather, plumage 86, 100, 123, 137, 145, 163, 205, 239, 266, 306, 347, 380.

**feþerhoma** *m.* plumage 280.

**finta** *m.* tail 295.

**fīras** *mpl.* men, human beings 3, 396, 535 ; *gen.* **fȳra** 492.

**firgenstrēam** *m.* ocean 100.

**fiþre** *n.* wing 297, 316, 652.

**flǣsc** *n.* flesh 221, 259, 535.

**flēogan** *sv.* 2 to fly 163, 322.

**flēon** *sv.* 2 to flee 460.

**flyht** *m.* flight 123, 340.

**flyhthwæt** *adj.* swift-flying 145, 335.

**fnǣst** *m.* breath, blast *15.*

**fōddor** *n.* food 259.

**fōdorþegu** *f.* sustenance 248.

**folc** *n.* people, crowd 322, 326.

**folcāgend** *m.* ruler of a nation, man 5.

**folde** *f.* earth 3, 8, 60, 74, 174, 197, 257, 396 ; land, region 29, 155, 352 ; soil, land 64 ; earth, mold 490.

**foldwæstm** *m.* fruit of the earth 654.

**foldwylm** *m.* spring, stream 64.

**folgian** *wv.* 2 to follow 591.

**for** *prep. w. dat.* for, as 344 ; on account of, because of 461.

**foran** *adv.* before, in front 292.

**forbēodan** *wv.* 2 to forbid, *pp. acc. sg. m.* **forbodene** 404.

**forberstan** *sv.* 2 to fail, be wanting 568.

**fore** *prep. w. dat.* before 600 *w. acc.* before 514.

**foregenga** *m.* forefather 437.

**foremihtig** *adj.* eminent in power 159.

**forgifan** *sv.* 5 to give, grant, bestow 377, 615 ; *pp.* **forgiefen** 175.

forgildan *sv.* 3 to recompense, requite 473.

forgrindan *sv.* 3 to destroy 227.

forgrīpan *sv.* 1 to seize 507.

forht *adj.* fearful, terrified 504.

forhtāfǣran *wv.* 1 to terrify 525.

forhycgan *wv.* 3 to scorn, despise 552.

forniman *sv.* 4 to destroy 268.

forst *m.* frost 15, 58, 248.

forswelan *sv.* 4 to burn, shrivel 532.

forð *adv.* always 455, 637; thenceforth 579.

forþon *adv.* hence, consequently 368, 411.

forðweard *adj.* abiding, lasting 569.

forþylman *wv.* 1 to envelop, wrap 284.

forweard *adj.* in front, forward 291.

fōt *m.* foot 276, 578; *nom. pl.* fōtas 311.

frǣtwe *fpl.* fruit 73, 150, 200, 257, 330, 335, 508, 610; *instr.* frǣtwum gloriously, splendidly 95, 309.

Frēa *m.* lord, God 578, 675.

frēcne *adj.* terrible, dangerous 390, 450.

Frēfrend *m.* comforter, God 422.

fremman *wv.* 1 to accomplish 470.

freoþu *f.* peace 597.

frōd *adj.* old, wise, experienced 154, 219, 426, 570; old, ancient 84.

from *prep. w. dat.* from, away from, out of 353, 524.

fromlīce *adv.* speedily 371.

fruma *m.* beginning 328; creator, God 377.

frymþ *m.f.* beginning 84, 197, 239, 280, 630, 637.

fugel *m.* bird 86, 100, 104, 121, 125, 155, 159, 163, 174, 201, 215, 257, 266, 291, 309, 311, 315, 322, 328, 330, 335, 352, 360, 387, 426, 466, 510, 529, 558, 574, 578, 585, 591, 597, 652; fugol 145.

fugeltimber *n.* young bird 236.

fugol *see* fugel.

ful *adj.* full 267.

fultum *m.* aid, help 390, 455, 646.

furþor *adv.* further, more 236.

fūs *adj.* ready, eager 208.

fyll *m.* death, dissolution 371.

fȳr *n.* fire 15, 215, 219, 276, 380, 490, 504, 525, 531, 545.

fȳras *see* fīras.

fȳrbæð *n.* bath of flame 437.

fyrndagas *mpl.* ancient days, time long past 570.

fyrngēar *npl.* past years 219.

fyrngesceap *n.* ancient decree 360.

fyrngesetu *npl.* ancient home 263.

fyrngeweorc *n.* ancient work 84, 95.

fyrstmearc *f.* appointed time, proper interval 223.

gǣdrian *wv.* 2 to gather 193.

gǣst *m.* spirit, soul 513, 519, 539, 544, 549, 593, 615.

garsecg *m.* ocean 289.

ge *conj.* and 523.

geador *adv.* together 285.

geaflas *mpl.* jaws 300.

gēar *n.* year 154, 258.

geard *m.* home, dwelling place 355, 578, 647.

gēardagas *mpl.* past days 384.

gearwian *wv.* 2 to make ready, prepare 189.

geascian *wv.* 2 to learn 393.

gebǣru *f.* song, voice 125.

gebed *n.* prayer 458.

gebēodan *sv.* 2 to offer 401.

gebīdan *sv.* 1 to expect, await 562; to attain, experience 152.

**geblissian** *wv.* 2 to bless, gladden 7, 140.

**geblondan** *sv.* 7 to mingle, mix 294.

**geblōwan** *sv.* 7 to bloom, flower 21, 27, 47, 155, 179, 240.

**gebod** *n.* behest, bidding 68.

**gebrēadian** *wv.* 2 to rejuvenate, restore 372.

**gebrecan** *sv.* 4 to destroy 80, 229.

**gebrēdian** *wv.* 2 to rejuvenate, restore 592.

**gebregd** *n.* vicissitude 57.

**gebringan** *sv.* 3 to bring, gather 271, 283.

**gebrosnian** *wv.* 2 to decay, putrefy 270.

**gebyrd** *f.* sex 360.

**gebyrgan** *wv.* 1 to taste 261.

**gebysgian** *wv.* 2 to trouble, afflict, weigh down 62, 162, 428.

**gecēosan** *sv.* 2 to choose, select 382, 388, 541, 593.

**geclingan** *sv.* 3 to contract 226.

**gecweðan** *sv.* 5 to speak 551.

**gecȳgan** *wv.* 1 to invoke 454.

**gecynd** *f.* nature, natural properties 252, 256 ; nature, kind, species 329, 387.

**gecynde** *n.* sex 356.

**gedǣlan** *wv.* 1 to diversify, variegate 295.

**gedāl** *n.* death, dissolution 651.

**gedēman** *wv.* 1 to ordain 147.

**gedryht** *f.* flock, company 348, 615, 635.

**geealdian** *wv.* 2 to grow old 427.

**geēawan** *wv.* 1 to manifest, be revealed 334.

**geendian** *wv.* 2 to end 500.

**gefær** *n.* expedition, journey 426.

**gefan** *sv.* 5 to give, 3 *sg. pres.* gefeð 319.

**gefēa** *m.* delight, happiness, joy 389, 400, 422, 569, 607 ; *acc. sg.* gefēon 248.

**gefēalic** *adj.* agreeable, joyous 510.

**gefēgan** *wv.* 1 to join, fit together 309.

**gefēon** *see* **gefēa.**

**gefēre** *adj.* accessible 4.

**gefōn** *sv.* 7 to seize, take, **hlyst gefēð** listens 143.

**gefrǣge** *n.* report, information 176.

**gefrǣge** *adj.* famous 3.

**gefrætwian** *wv.* 2 to adorn, embellish, accoutre 116, 239, 274, 585.

**gefremman** *wv.* 1 to do, accomplish, bring about 463, 495, 650.

**gefreogum** *see* **gefrige.**

**gefreoþian** *wv.* 2 to defend, protect 630.

**gefrige** *n.* information, knowledge, *instr. pl.* gefreogum 29.

**gefrignan** *sv.* 3 to learn, hear 1.

**gefylgan** *wv.* 1 to follow 347.

**gefyllan** *wv.* 1 to fill 627, 653.

**gegædrian** *wv.* 2 to gather 269, 512.

**gehealdan** *sv.* 7 to protect 45 ; to keep, observe 476.

**gehefgian** *wv.* 2 to burden (with age) 153.

**gehēgan** *wv.* 1 to hold 493.

**gehladan** *sv.* 6 to load 76.

**gehōn** *sv.* 7 to hang with, load with 38, 71.

**gehrēodan** *sv.* 2 to adorn 79.

**gehwā** *pron.* each, all, every 66, 195, *197*, 451, 464, 469, 487, 598, 603, 606 ; *dat. sg. f.* **gehwāre** 206, **gehwōre** 336.

**gehwæðer** *pron.* both, either 374.

**gehwylc** *pron.* each, all 110, 133, 185, 381, 460, 503, 522, 534, 615, 624.

**gehygd** *f.n.* thought, meditation 459.

**gehȳran** *wv.* 1 to obey 444 ; to hear, learn 548.

**gelǣdan** *wv.* 1 to lead, bring 244.

**gelēafa** *m.* belief, faith 479.

**gelīc** *adj.* like, similar 237, 387 ;
*superl.* 302, 424.

**gelīce** *adv.* like, alike 37, 601 ;
*superl.* 585.

**gelīcnes** *f.* likeness 230.

**gemāh** *adj.* malicious 595.

**gemearcian** *wv.* 2 to mark,
measure 146, 318.

**gemētan** *wv.* 1 to find, meet with
231, 429.

**gemong** *n.* multitude; **in gemonge**
*prep. w. dat.* in the middle of
265.

**gemōt** *n.* assembly 491.

**genēosian** *wv.* 2 to visit 351.

**genīwian** *wv.* 2 to renew, restore
279, 580.

**geofon** *n.* sea, ocean 118.

**geofona** *see* **giefu.**

**gēomor** *adj.* sad, sorrowful 139,
517, 556.

**gēomormōd** *adj.* sad, sorrowful
353, 412.

**geond** *prep. w. acc.* among,
through, throughout, in 82,
119, 323.

**geondfaran** *sv.* 6 to traverse 67.

**geondlācan** *sv.* 7 to flow through
70.

**geondwlītan** *sv.* 1 to survey 211.

**geong** *adj.* young 192, 258, 267,
433, 647 ; **giong** 355 ; perpetually new 624.

**georne** *adv.* eagerly 92, 101 ;
*comp.* 573.

**gesǣlig** *adj.* blessed, happy 350.

**gesceaft** *f.* heaven 660.

**gesceap** *n.* destiny, fate 210.

**gesceōðan** *sv.* 6 to harm, injure
400, 442.

**gescīnan** *sv.* 1 to illumine 118.

**gescyldan** *wv.* 1 to defend, protect 180.

**gescyppan** *sv.* 6 to create, fashion
84, 138, 197.

**gesēcan** *wv.* 1 to seek, visit, gain,
reach 156, 166, 264.

**gesēon** *sv.* 5 to see, behold 675.

**geset** *n.* abode, home 278, 417,
436.

**gesettan** *wv.* 1 to place, establish
10, 395.

**gesittan** *sv.* 5 to occupy 671.

**gesomnian** *wv.* 2 to gather 576.

**gestaþelian** *wv.* 2 to establish,
ordain 474.

**gestrȳnan** *wv.* 1 to gain, secure
392.

**geswigian** *wv.* 2 to bring to
silence 145.

**geswin** *n.* strain, melody 137.

**getimbran** *wv.* 1 to erect, construct 202, 430.

**geþēon** *sv.* 1 to exalt, advance
160 ; to girt, accoutre 649.

**geþonc** *m.n.* thought 552.

**geþrȳþan** *wv.* 1 to arm 486.

**geweaxan** *sv.* 7 to grow up 313.

**geweorðan** *sv.* 3 to come, become
41, 538.

**geweorðian** *wv.* 2 to mark out,
honour 551.

**gewīcian** *wv.* 2 to encamp, take
up one's abode 203.

**gewin** *n.* struggle 55.

**gewindæg** *m.* day of toil 612.

**gewītan** *sv.* 1 to go, depart, fly
97, 99, 122, 162, 320, 428, 554.

**gewitt** *n.* spirit, mind 191.

**gewlitegian** *wv.* 2 to embellish,
beautify 117.

**gewrit** *n.* writing, book 30, 313,
332, 655.

**gewunian** *wv.* 2 to inhabit, dwell
in 481.

**gewyrcan** *wv.* 1 to make, build,
bring to pass 469, 537.

**gewyrdan** *wv.* 1 to inflict damage,
do harm 19.

**gewyrtian** *wv.* 2 to perfume 543.

**gieddian** *wv.* 2 to sing 571.

**giedding** *f.* utterance, song 549.

**giefu** *f.* gift, grace, favour, en-
dowment 327, 557, 658 ; *gen.
pl.* **geofona** 267, 384, **gyfena**
624.

**gielt** *see* **gylt.**

**gīfre** *adj.* greedy, rapacious 507.

**gim** *m.* gem, jewel 92, 117, 183, 208, 289, 300, 303, 516.

**gin** *adv.* still 236.

**giong** *see* **geong.**

**glæd** *adj.* glad, joyous 593 ; brilliant, sparkling 92, 303 ; *superl.* 289.

**glædmōd** *adj.* glad-hearted 462, 519.

**glǣm** *m.* ray, beam 253.

**glæs** *n.* glass 300.

**glēaw** *adj.* wise, sage 29, 144.

**glēawmōd** *adj.* prudent, sagacious 571.

**glengan** *wv.* 1 to adorn, grace 606.

**glīdan** *wv.* 1 to glide 102.

**glīw** *n.* cheer, joy 139.

**God** *m.* God 36, 46, 91, 96, 281, 355, 403, 408, 461, 517, 565, 571, 619, 622, 657.

**gōd** *n.* bounty, good 615, 624.

**gōd** *adj.* good 462 ; *comp.* **sēlle** 417 ; *superl.* **sēlestan** 395, 620.

**Godbearn** *n.* son of God, Christ 647.

**gōddǣd** *f.* good deed, good works 669.

**gold** *n.* gold 506.

**goldfæt** *n.* gold-setting 303.

**gomel** *see* **gomol.**

**gomol** *adj.* old 154 ; **gomel** 258.

**gong** *m.* course 118.

**gongan** *sv.* 7 to go 519.

**grǣdig** *adj.* greedy 507.

**græswong** *m.* grassy plain 78.

**grēne** *adj.* green 13, 36, 78, *154*, 293, 298.

**grēot** *n.* earth (of the grave) 267, 556.

**grim** *adj.* fierce, grim 461.

**grund** *m.* earth, world 118, 498.

**gūdǣd** *f.* former deed 556.

**guma** *m.* human being, man 139, 570.

**gūðfreca** *m.* brave warrior 353.

**gyfl** *n.* morsel, food 410.

**gyfu** *see* **giefu.**

**gylt** *m.* sin 408 ; *acc. pl.* **gieltas** 461.

**gyrn** *m.f.n.* sorrow 410.

**gyrnan** *wv.* 1 to long for, yearn 462.

**habban** *wv.* 3 to have, hold, possess 1, 175, 393, 408, 569, 667.

**hād** *m.* form, shape, nature 372, 639.

**hādor** *adj.* radiant 212.

**hǣdre** *adv.* brightly, clearly 115, 619.

**hægl** *m.* hail 16, 60.

**hæle** *m.* man, warrior 554.

**Hǣlend** *m.* Saviour 616, 650.

**hǣlende** *adj.* redeeming, saving 590.

**hæleþ** *m.* man, warrior 49, 135, 170.

**hærfest** *m.* harvest 244.

**hǣtu** *f.* heat 17.

**hālig** *adj.* holy 73, 79, 81, 183, 206, 339, 399, 418, 421, 444, 447, 476, 515, 539, 619, 626, 641, 656.

**hals** *m.* neck 298.

**hām** *m.* home 244, 483, 593, 599.

**hasu** *adj.* pale grey 121.

**haswigfeðra** *wk. adj.* greyplumed 153.

**hāt** *adj.* hot 521, 613; *superl.* 209.

**hātan** *sv.* 7 to call, name 86, 173.

**hāte** *adv.* fervently 477.

**hē** *pron.* he, she, it ; *nom. sg. m.* **hē** 5, 142, 146, etc. ; *nom. sg. f.* **hēo** 413 ; *nom. acc. sg. n.* **hit** 84, 531 ; *acc. sg. m.* **hine** 106, 111, 281, etc. ; *gen. sg. m. n.* **his** 211, 262, 267, etc. ; *dat. sg. m. n.* **him** 88, 179, 189, etc. ; *nom. pl.* **hī**, **hȳ** 166, 247, 327, etc. ; *acc. pl.* **hī** 246, 395 ; *gen. pl.* **hyra** 405, 543 ; *dat. pl.* **him** 36, 39, 160, etc.

hēa *adj.* and *adv. see* hēah.

heafela *m.* head 604.

hēafod *n.* head 143, 293, 604.

hēah *adj.* high, lofty 429, 590, 626 ; hēa 447 ; *acc. sg. m.* hēanne 112, 171, 202, 391 ; *comp. nom. sg. f. n.* hērra 28.

hēah *adv.* high 23, 521, 641 ; hēa 32, 121.

Hēahcyning *m.* king in the highest 129, 446, 483.

hēahmōd *adj.* proud, noble 112.

hēahseld *n.* throne 619.

hēahsetl *n.* throne 515.

healdan *sv.* 7 to hold 391, 399, 457.

healf *f.* side 206, 336.

hēan *adj.* humiliated, abject 554.

hēannes *f.* height 631.

hēap *m.* multitude, troop 336.

heard *adj.* severe 58 ; *wk. nom. sg. m.* hearde 613.

hearm *adj.* malicious, fiendish 441.

hearpe *f.* harp 135.

heaþorōf *adj.* brave, valiant 228.

hebban *sv.* 6 to lift, raise 112.

heofon *m.* heaven 58, 73, 129, 131, 183, 391, 444, 446, 483, 521, 626, 641, 656 ; *gen. pl.* heofuna 631.

Heofoncyning *m.* King of heaven 616.

heofonrīce *n.* heaven, kingdom of heaven 12.

heofontungol *n.* star in the heavens, heavenly body 32.

heofumhrōf *m.* vault of heaven 173.

heolstor *n.* darkness 418.

heolstorcofa *m.* grave 49.

heonan *adv.* hence 1.

heoredrēorig *adj.* disconsolate, disheartened 217.

heorte *f.* heart, mind, spirit 552 ; *dat. sg.* eortan 477.

hēr *adv.* here 23, 31, 536, 638, 668.

hergan *wv.* 1 to praise 541, 616.

hettend *m.* enemy, devil 441.

hidercyme *m.* advent 421.

hige *m.* heart, soul, mind 477.

hindan *adv.* behind 293.

hindanweard *adj.* behind, at the back 298.

hinderweard *adj.* backward, slothful 314.

hīw *n.* colour, appearance, beauty 81, 291, 302, 311.

hlǣw *m.* mound 25.

hlēo *m.n.* protection 374, 429.

hleonian *wv.* 2 to tower, lean, incline 25.

hlēoþor *n.* melody, music 12, 131 ; speech 656.

hlēoþorcwide *m.* commandment, word 399.

hlēoþrian *wv.* 2 to sing, chant 539.

hlīfian *wv.* 2 to tower, rise 23, 32, 604.

hlinc *m.* hill 25.

hlūttor *adj.* bright, clear 183.

hlyn *m.* sound, tone 135.

hlyst *f.* listening, attention 143 ; *see* gefōn.

hof *n.* hall, house 228.

hold *adj.* gracious, well-disposed 446.

holmþracu *f.* turmoil of the sea 115.

holt *n.* grove, wood 73, 81, 429.

holtwudu *m.* wood, forest 171.

hond *f.* hand, power 441.

horn *m.* horn 134.

hrā *n.* corpse 228.

hrāwērig *adj.* weary in body, weary of life 554.

hrēmig *adj.* rejoicing, exultant 592 ; rēmig 126.

hrēoh *adj.* rough, angry, fierce 58, 217 ; *gen. pl. m.* hrēora 45.

hrēosan *sv.* 2 to fall 60.

hrīm *m.* hoarfrost 16, 60.

hring *m.* orb, ring, circle 305, 339.

hrōf *m.* roof 590.

**hryre** *m.* downpour 16 ; destruction, dissolution 645.

**hū** *adv.* how 342, 356, 359, 389.

**hungor** *m.* hunger 613.

**hūs** *n.* house, home 202, 212, 217.

**hwæþre** *adv.* yet, still, nevertheless 222, 366, 443, 640.

**hweorfan** *sv.* 3 to be active, move about 500 ; to pass, enter 519.

**hwīt** *adj.* white 298.

**hwonne** *conj.* when, until 93, 102, 114, 334.

**hwōpan** *sv.* 7 to threaten, menace 582.

**hygegǣlsa** *adj.* wanton, light-minded 314.

**hyht** *m.* hope 423, 480.

**hyhtlīce** *adv.* gaily 79.

**hȳran** *wv.* 1 to hear 129.

**ic** *pron.* I *nom. sg.* 1, 547, 552, etc. ; *dat. sg.* **mē** 567 ; *nom. pl.* **wē** 393, 573, 668, 670 ; *acc. pl.* **ūsic** 630 ; *dat. pl.* **ūs** 23, 29, 31, etc.

**īdig** *adj.* busy 407.

**īglond** *n.* island 9.

**ilca** *pron.* the same 379.

**in** *prep. w. dat.* in, on, upon 107, 168, 201, etc. ; *prep. w. acc.* in, into, to, throughout 77, 139, 200, etc.

**indryhto** *f.* blessing 198.

**innan** *adv.* within 200, 301.

**Iōb** *m.* Job 549.

**iū** *adv.* formerly, long ago 41.

**lācan** *sv.* 7 to fly, swing 316.

**lǣdan** *wv.* 1 to lead 345 ; *pp.* **lǣdaþ** 491 ; to carry, take 577.

**lǣne** *adj.* transitory, fleeting 220, 456, 481, 489, 505.

**lǣs** *adv. conj.* ; **þȳ lǣs** lest 246.

**lǣþþu** *f.* harm, injury 582.

**lāf** *f.* remains, leavings 269, 272, 276, 376, 575.

**lagu** *m.* sea, water 101.

**laguflōd** *m.* river, water 70.

**lagustrēam** *m.* river 62.

**lām** *n.* clay, dust 555.

**lār** *f.* doctrine, lore 476.

**lāst** *m.* trace, track ; **on lāste** behind 440.

**late** *adv.* slowly, sluggishly 316.

**lāþ** *adj.* evil (one), devil 53.

**lāðgenīðla** *m.* enemy, persecutor 50.

**lēaf** *n.* leaf 39.

**lēafscead** *n. f.* leafy shade 205.

**leahtor** *m.* iniquity, sin 456, 518.

**lēan** *n.* recompense, reward 386, 475.

**lēas** *adj.* deprived of, without 454.

**leccan** *wv.* 1 to irrigate 64.

**leger** *n.* disease 56.

**lencten** *m.* spring 254.

**lēodfruma** *m.* prince 345.

**lēodscype** *m.* land 582.

**lēof** *adj.* dear, beloved 345, 479, 561.

**lēoflīc** *adj.* lovely 440.

**lēoht** *n.* light 116, 288, 508, 563, 596, 607.

**lēoht** *adj.* light, agile 317 ; fair, clear, pure 479, 661.

**lēoma** *m.* light, gleam, ray 103, 116.

**leomu, leomum** *see* **lim.**

**leornere** *m.* scholar 424.

**lēoð** *n.* song 547.

**leoþucræftig** *adj.* nimble, with active limbs 268.

**līc** *n.* body 205, 268, 513, 523, 563, 584, 645, 651.

**licgan** *sv.* 5 to be at rest 182.

**līchoma** *m.* body 220, 489, 518.

**līcian** *wv.* 2 to please, gratify 517

**līf** *n.* life 53, 150, 151, 191, 220, 254, 365, 367, 370, 381, 417, 434, 456, 481, *513*, 533, 561, 572, 607, 645, 649, 651, 661.

**lifgan** *wv.* 3 to live 596, 672.

**līg** *m.* fire, flame 39, 218, 268, 434, 505, 533.

**līgbryne** *m.* burning, fire 577.

**līgþracu** *f.* fire's violence 225, 370.

**līhtan** *see* **lȳhtan.**

**lim** *n.* limb; *acc. pl.* **leomu** 513 ; *dat. pl.* **leomum** 649.

**liss** *f.* joy, bliss 150, 563, 672.

**līxan** *wv.* 1 to gleam, shine, glisten 33, 94, 290, 299, 604.

**lōcian** *wv.* 2 to look 101.

**lof** *m.n.* praise 617, 634, 661, 676.

**lofian** *wv.* 2 to praise 337, 561.

**lond** *n.* land 2, 20, 28, 50, 70, 116, 150, 166 ; earth, world 508.

**londwela** *m.* riches of the world 505.

**long** *adj.* long 440, 555 ; enduring, lasting 607.

**long** *adv.* long 481.

**longe** *adv.* long 489.

**lūcan** *sv.* 2 to knit together, unite 225.

**lufian** *wv.* 2 to love 478.

**lyft** *m.f.n.* air 123, 316, 340 ; wind 62 ; sky, heaven 39, 101.

**lygeword** *n.* falsehood, lie 547.

**lȳhtan** *wv.* 1 to shine, give light 187 ; 3 *sg. pres.* **līhteð** 587.

**lyre** *m.* loss 53.


**mæg** *v.* I can, am able 14, 113, 134, 179, 347, 448, 561, 573, 581, 594.

**mægen** *n.* strength, power, might 471, 625.

**mægenþrym** *m.* heavenly host 665.

**mǣran** *wv.* 1 to glorify, extol 338, 344.

**mǣre** *adj.* glorious 165, 633, 660 ; *superl.* 119.

**mǣrsian** *wv.* 2 to celebrate 617.

**mǣrðu** *f.* glory, renown 472.

**mǣst** *see* **micel.**

**mæþel** *n.* assembly, judgement 538.

**mān** *n.* evil, sin 633.

**māndǣd** *f.* evil deed 457.

**mānfremmende** *adj.* wicked, sinful 6.

**marmstān** *m.* marble 333.

**meagol** *adj.* powerful 338.

**meaht** *f.* power, might 6, 10, 79, 499, 617, 640, 647 ; **miht** 583.

**meahtig** *adj.* mighty 538 ; *wk. nom. sg. m.* **meahta** 377, **mihtiga** 496.

**mearcian** *wv.* 2 to inscribe, write 333.

**meledēaw** *m.* honey dew, nectar 260.

**mengu** *f.* multitude, a great many 420.

**meord** *f.* reward 472.

**Meotud** *m.* lord, creator, God 6, 176, 443, 457, 471, 524, 660 ; **Meotod** 358 ; *dat. sg.* **Metude** 617.

**mereflōd** *m.* flood 42.

**mētan** *wv.* 1 to find 247.

**mete** *m.* food 260.

**Metud** *see* **Meotud.**

**mēþe** *adj.* weary, disconsolate 422.

**micel** *adj.* much, great 189, 432, 625 ; *superl.* **mǣst** 167, 462, 618.

**mid** *adv.* also, besides 532.

**mid** *prep. w. dat.* with, by, among 8, 23, 31, etc. ; with, together with 215, 523, 584, etc. ; *w. acc.* with, together with 483, 560.

**midd** *adj.* middle, midst 262, 340.

**middangeard** *m.* world, earth 4, 42, 119, 157, 323, 640, 665.

**middel** *m.* middle 65.

**miht, mihtig** *see* **meaht, meahtig.**

**milde** *adj.* gracious, merciful 538, 657.

**mīn** *adj.* 176, 553, 563.

**mirce** *adj.* dark, gloomy 457.

**mōd** *n.* mind, heart, spirit 446, 471, 657.

**mōdig** *adj.* spirited, noble 10, 262, 338.

**moldærn** *n.* grave 564.

**molde** *f.* land 10 ; earth 66, 260, 496.

**moldgræf** *n.* grave 524.

**molsnian** *wv.* 2 to decay 564.

**mon** *m.* man, person 128, 157, 173, 323, 358, 496, 544 ; one 243.

**mōnaþ** *m.* month 66.

**moncynn** *n.* mankind 176, 377, 422.

**monig** *adj.* many, all 443, 491 ; *dat. pl. m.* **mongum** 4, 323 ; **monegum** 170, 521.

**monn** *see* **mon.**

**mōt** *v.* I may, may be allowed 148, 190, 361, 383, 433, 436, 516, 559, 668 ; 1 *pl. pres.* **motum** 670.

**mund** *f.* hand 333.

**munt** *m.* mountain 21.


**nǣdre** *f.* serpent, devil 413.

**nǣfre** *adv.* never 38, 88, 567.

**nǣnig** *pron.* none, no 397.

**nǣs** *see* **wesan.**

**nān** *pron.* none, no 51, 449.

**ne** *adv.* not 14, 22, 25, etc.

**ne** *conj.* neither, nor 14, 15, 16, etc.

**nēah** *adv.* near 192.

**nēan** *adv.* from near 326.

**nearwe** *adv.* grievously 413.

**nebb** *n.* beak, bill 299.

**nemnan** *wv.* 1 to name, call 397.

**nemne** *conj.* except that, save that 260.

**nēobed** *n.* deathbed 553.

**nēod** *f.* desire 189, 432.

**neorxnawong** *m.* paradise 397.

**nēotan** *sv.* 2 *w. gen.* to enjoy 149, 361, 384.

**neoþan** *adv.* beneath 307.

**Nergend** *m.* Saviour 498.

**nest** *n.* nest 189, 215, 227, 432, 451, 469, 530, 553.

**niht** *f.* night 98, 147, 262, 478.

**niman** *sv.* 4 to take, snatch away 380, 485.

**nioþoweard** *adj.* below 299.

**nis** *see* **wesan.**

**nīþ** *m.* hatred, malice, evil 400, 413, 451, 469.

**nīwe** *adj.* new 266, 400, 431.

**nō** *adv.* not at all, by no means, no 72, 80, 157, 259.

**noma** *m.* name 174.

**norþan** *adv.* from the north 324.

**nū** *adv.* now 447, 470, 583.


**ō** *adv.* ever, always 72 ; **ōo** 25 ; *see* **ā.**

**of** *prep. w. dat.* of, out of, from 65, 66, 109, etc.

**ofer** *prep. w. acc.* over, across 94, 101, 103, etc. ; throughout 4, 197, 331, 498 ; beyond, surpassing 330, 480 ; against 403, 411 ; *w. dat.* above, over 588, 604, 641.

**oferhlīfian** *wv.* 2 to rise above 121.

**ofermægen** *n.* force, irresistible power 249.

**ofest** *f.* haste 190.

**ofett** *n.* fruit 77.

**ofgiefan** *sv.* 5 to forsake, relinquish 412, 426.

**oft** *adv.* often 11, 108, 261, 442.

**on** *prep. w. dat.* in, on, among, upon 2, 30, 50, etc. ; by, with 484, 578 ; at 244, 246 ; *w. acc.* in, on, upon, into 74, 97, 98, etc.

**onǣlan** *wv.* 1 to enkindle, inflame 216, 503.

**onbregdan** *sv.* 3 *w. dat.* to lift, move 143.

**onbryrdan** *wv.* 1 to inspire 126, 550.

**ond** *conj.* and 20, 37, 91, etc.

**ondleofen** *f.* food, sustenance 243.

**ōnettan** *wv.* 1 to hasten 217 ; to be (well) employed 455.

**onfōn** *sv.* 7 to take, receive, gain 159, 192, 433, 533, 645.

**ongēan** *prep. w. dat.* towards 91.

**ongieldan** *sv.* 3 to pay the penalty, requite 410.

**ongietan** *sv.* 5 to understand 573.

**onginnan** *sv.* 3 to begin 188, 224.

**ongyn** *n.* beginning 638.

**onhǣtan** *wv.* 1 to ignite 212.

**onhlīdan** *sv.* 1 to open 12, 49.

**onlīc** *adj.* like, *superl.* 312.

**onlīce** *adv.* similarly, in like manner 242.

**onsāwan** *sv.* 7 to sow 253.

**onspringan** *sv.* 3 to spring up 63.

**onsund** *adj.* flourishing 20 ; unscathed 44.

**onsȳn** *f.* lack, want 55, 398.

**onsȳn** *f.* face 600.

**ontȳnan** *wv.* 1 to open, disclose 423.

**onwæcnan** *wv.* 1 to awake, rise again ; 3 *sg. pres.* **onwæcned** 648.

**onwald** *m.* power 663 ; *see* **anwald**.

**onwendan** *wv.* 1 to change 82.

**ōo** *see* **ō**.

**open** *adj.* open 11 ; manifest 509.

**organa, organe** *m.f.* organ 136.

**orþonc** *m.* art, skill 304.

**oð** *prep. w. acc.* till, until 47, 490.

**oðēawan** *wv.* 1 to appear, be manifest 322.

**ōþer** *pron.* other 343.

**oðflēogan** *sv.* 2 to fly away 347.

**oðscūfan** *sv.* 2 to hasten away 168.

**oþþæt** *conj.* until 141, 151, 166, etc.

**oþþe** *conj.* or 300.


**pēa** *m.* peacock 312.

**ræfnan** *wv.* 1 to suffer 643.

**rēmig** *see* **hrēmig**.

**rēn** *m.* rain 14, 246.

**reord** *f.* melody, voice 128, 338.

**reordian** *wv.* 2 to discourse, speak 550, 632.

**rīce** *n.* realm, region, kingdom 156, 664.

**rinnan** *sv.* 3 to run, pass, *pp.* **urnen** 364.

**rōd** *f.* cross 643.

**roder** *m.* sky, heaven 14, 664.

**rūm** *adj.* extensive, spacious 14.

**ryht** *n.* equity, justice 494 ; **on ryht** justly, by right 664.

**ryhtfremmende** *adj.* righteous 632.

**ryp** *n.* harvest 246.


**sacu** *f.* strife 54.

**sǣ** *m.* sea 103.

**sǣd** *n.* seed 253.

**sǣgan** *wv.* 1 to cause to rest 142.

**sǣl** *m.f.* delight, happiness 140.

**sār** *adj.* dire, grievous 369.

**sārlīc** *adj.* grievous 406.

**sārwracu** *f.* misery, tribulation 54, 382.

**sāwel** *f.* soul 488, 498, 523, 540, 566, 584, 589.

**scad** *n.* secret shelter, refuge 168 ; shadow, *dat. sg.* **sceade** 234, *acc. pl.* **sceadu** 210.

**scanca** *m.* leg 310.

**scead** *see* **scad**.

**sceal** *v.* I must, ought, shall 90, 250, 378, 412, 563, 643.

**scearplīce** *adv.* abruptly 168.

**scēat** *m.* region 3, 396.

**scēawian** *wv.* 2 to see, behold 327.

**sceððan** *sv.* 6 to harm, injure 39, 88, 180, 449, 595.

**scīnan** *sv.* 1 to shine 183, 210, 515, 589.

**scīr** *adj.* bright, glorious 234, 308.

**scolu** *f.* host, throng 560.

**scomu** *f.* dishonour, shame 502.

scūr *m.* shower 246.

scyld *m.* crest 308 ; shield, protection 463.

scyld *f.* evil, sin 180.

scyldwyrcende *adj.* sinful 502.

scyll *f.* shell 234 ; scale 310.

scȳne *adj.* brilliant, resplendent 300, 308, 591.

Scyppend *m.* creator 327, 630.

se, sē *adj. pron.* he, that, who, which, the ; *nom. sg. m.* se, sē 3, 7, 9, etc. ; *nom. sg. f.* sēo 98, 120, 141, etc. ; *nom. acc. sg. n.* þæt 9, 13, 20, etc. ; *acc. sg. m.* ðone 85, 173, 281, etc. ; *acc. sg. f.* þā 10, 190, 450, etc. ; *gen. sg. m. n.* þæs 65, 107, 122, etc. ; *gen. dat. sg. f.* þǣre 66, 90, 231, etc. ; *dat. sg. m. n.* þām 50, 78, 104, etc. ; *instr. sg. m. n.* þon 238, 262, 424, þȳ 573, 644 ; *nom. acc. pl.* þā 35, 71, 193, etc. ; *gen. pl.* þāra 31, 138 ; *dat. pl.* þām 8, 76, 109, etc. ; *see* ǣr þon, þæs, þȳ lǣs.

sealt *adj.* salty 120.

searo *n.* care 269 ; deceit, wile 419.

searolīce *adv.* cunningly, artistically 297.

sēcan *wv.* 1 to seek, visit, repair to 275, 278, 320, 349, 436, 458, 524, 671 ; to seek, endure 416.

secgan *wv.* 3 to relate, declare 313, 425, 655.

self *see* sylf.

sēlle, sēlest *see* gōd.

sellīc *adj.* rare, wonderful 606 ; unique *comp.* 329.

sendan *wv.* 1 to send 488.

seomian *wv.* 2 to abide, remain 19.

seonoþ *m.* council, assembly 493.

setl *n.* seat 439.

settan *wv.* 1 to set, place 282 ; to ordain 328.

sib *f.* bliss, peace 601, 622.

sibgedryht *f.* company, heavenly host 618.

sīd *adj.* broad, wide, spacious 156, 498 ; *acc. sg. m.* sīðne 103.

sīde *adv.* far, wide 467.

sīdweg *m.* distant part 337.

sīgan *sv.* 1 to fly in, press in 337.

sigewong *m.* plain, field of victory 33.

sigor *m.* victory 329, 464, 493, 675.

sigorfæst *adj.* victorious, triumphant 282.

sincaldu *f.* perpetual cold 17.

sindrēam *m.* perpetual bliss 385.

singan *sv.* 3 to sing, chant, hymn 124, 140, 617, 676 ; 3 *sg. pres.* singad 635.

sittan *sv.* 5 to sit 208.

sīð *see* sīd.

sīþ *m.* time 69, 106, 146, 464 ; journey, passage, march 90, 114, 208, 220, 440, 555.

sīþian *wv.* 2 to journey 584.

siþþan *adv.* later, afterwards, then 111, 385, 409, 577, 579.

siþþan *conj.* when, as soon as 117, 224 ; since 129.

slǣp *m.* sleep 56.

smiþ *m.* goldsmith 304.

smylte *adj.* serene 33.

snāw *m.* snow 14, 248.

snel *see* snell.

snell *adj.* swift, speedy, nimble 123 ; snel 163, 317, 347.

snūde *adv.* quickly 488.

snyttrucræft *m.* prudence, wisdom 622.

solere *m.* a sunny room, sunlounge 204.

somnian *wv.* 2 to collect, gather 193, 269, 467 ; to assemble 324 ; to compose 547.

somod *adv.* together 513, 584 ; also 629.

sōna *adv.* soon, quickly ; sōna swā as soon as 120.

song *m.* song 337, 540.

songcræft *m.* musical creation 132.

**sorg** *f.* sorrow, anxiety 56, 611.

**sorgful** *adj.* sorrowful, *comp.* 417.

**sōð** *adj.* true 622.

**Sōðcyning** *m.* true king 329, 493.

**sōðfæst** *adj.* faithful, righteous, blessed 523, 540, 587, 589, 606, 635.

**spēd** *f.* fulness, abundance 394, 640.

**spēdig** *adj.* abounding, rich 10.

**spelboda** *m.* prophet 571.

**splott** *m.* splotch, spot 296.

**stān** *m.* stone, precious stone 302.

**stānclif** *n.* cliff, crag 22.

**stapelian** *wv.* 2 to establish 130.

**stēap** *adj.* steep 22.

**stearc** *adj.* piercing, stark 302.

**stefn** *f.* voice 135, 542 ; sound 497.

**stenc** *m.* odour, fragrance, spice 8, 81, 206, 586, 659.

**stīgan** *sv.* 1 to ascend, rise 520, 542.

**stille** *adv.* still 185.

**stondan** *sv.* 6 to stand 22, 36, 45, 78, 185 ; to endure, remain 89, 181.

**storm** *m.* storm 185.

**stōw** *f.* place, spot 169.

**strēam** *m.* stream, water 120.

**strenðu** *f.* might, power 625.

**strong** *adj.* strong 86, 99, 161.

**stȳman** *wv.* 1 to fume, reek 213.

**sum** *pron.* part(ly) 296 ; some, certain 315.

**sumer** *m.* summer 37, 209.

**sumes** *adv.* somewhat 242.

**sunbearo** *m.* sunny grove 33.

**sunbeorht** *adj.* bright with sunlight 278, 436.

**sundplega** *m.* bath 111.

**sunne** *f.* sun 17, 90, 120, 141, 209, 253, 288, 305, 532, 579, 587, 601.

**sunu** *m.* son 375, 406.

**sūþan** *adv.* from the south 186, 324.

**sūðrodor** *m.* southern sky 141.

**swā** *adv.* thus, so, in like manner 47, 104, 140, etc. ; then 121 ; very, exceedingly 125 ; also 405 ; **swā þēah** nevertheless, yet 565.

**swā** *conj.* as, even as, just 23, 29, 36, etc. ; when 41, 322 ; like 300, 315, 558 ; **sōna swā** as soon as 120.

**swæcc** *m.* odour 214.

**swæs** *adj.* own dear 375.

**swan** *m.* swan 137.

**swār** *adj.* dire, sore 56 ; heavy 315.

**swēg** *m.* melody, sound 131, 618.

**swegl** *n.* heaven, sky 103, 114, 186, 199, 208, 288, 374, 467, 635 ; sun 124, 212.

**sweglcondel** *f.* heaven's candle, sun 108.

**swēglēoþor** *n.* melody 137.

**swelgan** *sv.* 3 to swallow 507.

**swēora** *m.* neck 305.

**swēte** *adj.* sweet 214, 652 ; *comp.* 132 ; *superl.* 193, *acc. sg. m.* **swētes** 199.

**sweþrian** *wv.* 2 to die down, go out 229 ; to diminish 608.

**swift** *adj.* swift 317.

**swigian** *wv.* 2 to be silent, 3 *sg. pres.* **swīað** 142.

**swinsian** *wv.* 2 to make melody, sing 124, 140, 618.

**swīþe** *adv.* very 317.

**swol** *n.* heat, fire, flame 214, 269.

**swongor** *adj.* sluggish 315.

**swylc** *pron.* such as 239.

**swylce** *adv. conj.* as if 233 ; like, as 235, 305.

**swyltcwalu** *f.* agony of death 369.

**swylthwīl** *f.* hour of death 350, 566.

**sylf** *pron.* self, own 111, 199, 282, 382, 530, 532 ; **self** 374 ; alone 204.

**symbel** *n.* banquet, feast 406.

**symle** *adv.* always, for ever, ever 76, 108, 146, etc.

**synn** *f.* sin, evil 54, 242.
**synnig** *adv.* sinful 523.
**Syrware** *mpl.* Syrians 166.

**tācen** *n.* sign, token 96, 254, 450 ; significance, interpretation 510, 574.
**tān** *m.* twig 430.
**tapur** *m.* taper, light 114.
**telga** *m.* bough, branch 76, 188.
**tēon** *sv.* 2 to make, undertake 440.
**tēonlīce** *adv.* grievously 407.
**tīd** *f.* time 77, 209, 390, 450, 509, 517 ; hour 146, 334.
**tiht** *m.* motion, march 525.
**tilgan** *wv.* 2 to strive for 472.
**tīma** *m.* time 246.
**timbran** *wv.* 1 to build 188.
**tīrēadig** *adj.* blessed, glorious 106.
**tīrfæst** *adj.* glorious 69, 574.
**tīrmeahtig** *adj.* almighty 175.
**tō** *prep. w. dat.* to 60, 191, 226, etc. ; for, as 139, 198, 243, etc. ; **tō ealdre** for ever 40, 83, 562, 594 ; at 195 ; **tō ēacan** besides, likewise 285 ; *w. inf.* to 275.
**tōgædre** *adv.* together 225.
**tōgēanes** *prep. w. dat.* towards, against, for 11, 579 ; **tōhēanes** 124, 421.
**tōhēanes** *see* **tōgēanes**.
**torht** *adj.* bright, glorious 28, 96, 200, 574.
**tōþ** *m.* tooth, *nom. pl.* **tōþas** 407.
**tōwegan** *sv.* 5 to disperse 184.
**trēo** *n.* tree, wood 76, 175, 200, 643.
**tū** *num.* two 652.
**tungol** *n.* star 93, 96, 119.
**turf** *f.* turf, soil 66, 349.
**twelf** *num.* twelve 28, 69, 106, 146.

**þā** *adv.* then 43, 395.
**þā** *conj.* when 66, 281, 413, 466.

**ðǣr** *adv.* there 11, 14, 21, etc.
**þǣr** *conj.* where 157, 327, 397, etc.
**þæs** *adv. conj.* as, in respect of which, because of which 313, 409, 472 ; **þæs þe** as 424 ; because 476.
**þæt** *conj.* that, in order that, so that 148, 168, 177, etc.
**þætte** *conj.* that 1, 69.
**þe** *indecl. pron.* who, which, that 31, 138, 196, etc.
**þe** *conj.* or 357 ; because 369, 568 ; in that 410.
**þēah** *conj.* although 380, 563, 638, 642 ; **swā þēah** nevertheless, yet 565.
**þearlīc** *adj.* terrible 644.
**ðēaw** *m.* custom, practice 444.
**þeccan** *wv.* 1 to engulf, invest, enfold 42, 216, 365 ; to cover, deck 249.
**þegn** *m.* servant, attendant 165, 288, 388.
**þenden** *conj.* while, as long as 89, 181, 398.
**þēod** *f.* nation, people 160, 341.
**þēoden** *m.* leader, lord, God 68, 165, 605.
**þēow** *m.* servant 165.
**þes** *pron.* this, that, these, those 139, 151, 321, etc.
**þicgan** *sv.* 5 to seize upon, take, eat 219, 259, 402, 410, 505.
**þīn** *pron.* thy, thine, your 628.
**þonan** *adv.* thence 113, 415, 554.
**þonc** *m.* thought 144 ; thanks, gratitude 623.
**þonne** *adv.* then 99, 125, 142, etc.
**þonne** *conj.* when 48, 182, 208, etc. ; than 31, 128.
**þrāg** *f.* time, season 68, 160.
**þrēat** *m.* troop, throng 341, 501.
**þridda** *adj.* third 644.
**þringan** *sv.* 3 to crowd, throng, press 163, 336, 501.
**þrīst** *adj.* bold, brave 144.
**þriwa** *adv.* thrice 144.

þrym _m._ onset 41 ; glory, majesty 541, 605 ; lord 628.

þrymlīce _adv._ gloriously 68, 514.

þrymsittende _adj._ throned in majesty 623.

þrȳþ _f._ raging 184 ; host 326.

þū _pron._ thou, you 622, 623, 630.

þurh _prep. w. acc._ through, in, by, with, by reason of, on account of 6, 30, 46, etc.

þurst _m._ thirst 613.

þus _adv._ thus 482, 570, 621, 632.

þūsend _n._ thousand 364.

þūsende _f._ thousand 151.

þȳ lǣs _conj._ lest 246.

ufan _adv._ above 308.

ufeweard _adj._ above, on the upper side 299.

unbryce _adj._ eternal 642.

uncyst _f._ sin 526.

under _prep. w. dat._ under, beneath 14, 27, 32, etc. ; _w. acc._ under, beneath 97, 101, 374.

ungewyrded _adj._ uninjured 181.

unmǣte _adj._ infinite 625.

unrǣd _m._ evil counsel 403.

unsmēþe _adj._ rough, rugged 26.

unwemme _adj._ inviolate 46.

ūp _adv._ up, upwards 93, 102, 289, 511.

ūplǣdende _adj._ lofty, tall 178.

ūplīc _adj._ celestial, heavenly 392, 663.

uppe _adv._ above, on high 629.

urnen _see_ rinnan.

ūs, ūsic _see_ ic.

ūser _pron._ our, _nom. acc. pl. m._ ūsse 414, 438.

ūt _adv._ out 233.

ūtan _adv._ around, about 164, 204, 530 ; outside, on the outside 301.

wǣdl _f._ poverty, want 55.

wǣg _m._ wave, billow 45.

wælgīfre _adj._ murderous 486.

wælrēaf _n._ corpse, carnage 273.

wǣpen _n._ weapon 486.

wæsm _see_ wæstm.

wæstm _m.f.n._ fruit, crop 34, 72, 250, 255, 466 ; _acc. pl._ wæsmas 243 ; form, growth, proportion 237, 332 ; body, flesh 580.

wæter _n._ water 41, 61, 65, 184.

wāfian _wv._ 2 to gaze at _342._

Waldend _m._ ruler, lord 464, 631.

wāþ _f._ flight 99, 161.

waþema _m._ wave 97.

wē _see_ ic.

weald _m._ wood, forest 13.

weallende _adj._ surging, beating 477.

weard _m._ guardian, protector 152.

weardian _wv._ 2 to hold possession of, inhabit 85, 161, 168, 172, 448.

wearm _adj._ warm, hot 18, 187.

wearmian _wv._ 2 to glow, become hot 213.

wēatācen _n._ sign of woe 51.

weaxan _sv._ 7 to be born, grow, increase 232, 234.

weccan _wv._ 1 to waken 255.

weder _n._ weather 18, 57, 182.

wedercondel _f._ sun, candle in the sky 187.

wel _adv._ well, rightly _443,_ 516.

wela _m._ riches, wealth 55, 149.

weldǣd _f._ good deed 543.

wēn _f._ hope 567.

wēnan _wv._ 1 _w. gen._ to imagine 546.

wendan _wv._ 1 to turn, change 191.

weorc _n._ deed, act, work 386, 475, 527, 598, 659.

weord _see_ word.

weored _see_ weorod.

weorod _n._ people, host, company 187 ; _instr. sg._ werede 596 ; _gen. pl._ weoruda 465, 565 ; _dat. pl._ weoredum 588.

weorþan _sv._ 3 to be, become 49, 80, 142, 211, 240, 257, 304,

364, 372, 378, 404, 407, 417, 445, 503, 564.

**weorþian** *wv.* 2 to honour 343.

**weorŏmynd** *f.n.* honour 636.

**weorud** *see* **weorod**.

**wer** *m.* man 331, 394 ; male sex 357.

**wered** *see* **weorod**.

**werian** *wv.* 1 to apparel, clothe 596.

**wērigmōd** *adj.* weary in soul 428.

**wesan** *v.* to be, exist *inf.* 165, 435 ; 2 *sg. pres.* **eart** 630 ; 3 *sg. pres.* **is** 1, 5, 7, etc. ; **biŏ** 11, 37, 82, etc. ; **bēoþ** 96, 116, 474 ; **weseŏ** 373 ; 3 *pl. pres.* **sindon** 71, 297, 310, etc. ; **bēoŏ** 184, 255, 489, etc. ; **sind** 359, 465, 528 ; 3 *sg. pret.* **wæs** 239, 280, 379, 397 ; 3 *pl. pret.* **wæron** 443 ; 3 *sg. pres. subj.* **sī** 622 ; **sȳ** 623, 661 ; 3 *sg. pret. subj.* **wǣre** 639 ; *negative* 3 *sg. pres.* **nis** 3, 50, 314 ; 3 *sg. pret.* **næs** 637.

**west** *adv.* westward 162.

**westan** *adv.* from the west 325.

**westdǣl** *m.* western part 97.

**wēste** *adj.* deserted 169.

**wēsten** *m.n.* waste, wilderness, desert 161, 201.

**weþel** *f.* poverty 612.

**wīc** *n.* house, home, dwelling 448, 470, 474, 611.

**wīcstōw** *f.* dwelling-place 468.

**wīde** *adv.* wide, widely 467.

**wīf** *n.* woman 394.

**wīfhād** *m.* female sex 357.

**wiga** *m.* warrior 486.

**wiht** *f.* anything, aught 26, 179, 611 ; *instr. sg.* **wihte** in any way 19, 448.

**wilde** *adj.* wild 201, 343, 466, 529.

**wile** *see* **wille**.

**wilgedryht** *f.* joyful retinue 342.

**Wilgiefa** *m.* ruler, lord, king 465.

**willa** *m.* will, desire 149, 470 ; choice 537 ; joy, delight 565.

**wille** *v.* I will, wish 164, 399 ; 3 *sg. pres.* **wile** 472, 492.

**willsele** *m.* pleasant hall 213.

**willwong** *m.* delightful plain 89.

**wilsum** *adj.* delicious 109.

**wind** *m.* wind 182.

**windig** *adj.* wind-driven 61.

**winter** *m.* winter 37, 245 ; year 152, 162, 363, 420, 428, 580.

**wintergewǣde** *n.* winter garment 250.

**wintergeweorp** *n.* winter storm 57.

**winterscūr** *m.* wintry shower 18.

**wīsdōm** *m.* wisdom 30.

**wīse** *f.* fact, condition 359.

**wist** *f.* food 245.

**witan** *v.* to know 355, 357, 369.

**wīte** *n.* torture, torment 644.

**wītedōm** *m.* prophecy 548.

**wītga** *m.* prophet, sage 30.

**wiŏ** *prep. w. dat.* against 44, 451, 469.

**wlītan** *wv.* 1 to look, gaze 341.

**wlite** *m.* beauty, brightness, countenance 75, 332, 609.

**wlitig** *adj.* delightful, beautiful 7, 72, 203, 318, 439, 516, 588, 598, 666 ; *comp.* 132.

**wlitige** *adv.* brightly 543.

**wlitigfæst** *adj.* changeless in beauty 105.

**wlonc** *adj.* proud, stately 100.

**wolcen** *n.* cloud 27, 61, 184, 247.

**womb** *f.* body, belly 307.

**won** *adj.* dark, black 99.

**wong** *m.* plain 7, 13, 19, 43, 149, 281, 320, 363, 418, 439.

**wonian** *wv.* 2 to fade 72.

**wōp** *m.* weeping, lamentation 51.

**word** *n.* word 398, 411, 551, 655, 659 ; *instr. pl.* **weordum** 425.

**worn** *m.* multitude, throng 343.

**woruld** *f.* world 41, 89, 117, 130, 139, 181, 211, 386, 501 ; age 662, **þurh woruld worulda** for ever 662.

**woruldgestrēon** *n.* worldly treasure, riches of earth 255.

**woruldwela** *m.* worldly possession 480.

**wōðcræft** *m.* song 127 ; poetic skill 548.

**wracu** *f.* vengeance 51.

**wræchwīl** *f.* period of exile 527.

**wrǣtlīc** *adj.* beauteous 63, 307.

**wrǣtlīce** *adv.* splendidly 75 ; wonderfully 294, 367, 378.

**wraðu** *f.* support, help 247.

**wrenc** *m.* melody, song 133.

**wrīdian** *wv.* 2 to thrive, flourish 27, 237.

**writ** *n.* writing, book 425.

**wrītan** *sv.* 1 to write, compose 548.

**wrixlan** *wv.* 1 to sing 127 ; to variegate, *pp.* **wrixleð** 294.

**wrōht** *m.f.* misfortune 612.

**wudu** *m.* wood, forest 37, 65, 85.

**wudubēam** *m.* tree 75.

**wudubearo** *m.* grove 152, 169.

**wudublēd** *f.* forest fruit 194.

**wuduholt** *n.* wood, forest 34, 362.

**wuldor** *n.* glory 117, 130, 439, 475, 516, 542, 567, 588, 598, 628, 662 ; *instr. sg.* **wuldre** gloriously 318, 551, 609, 666.

**Wuldorcyning** *m.* King of glory 196, 420, 537.

**wundor** *n.* wonder, marvel, miracle 394 ; *instr. pl.* **wundrum** wondrously, strangely 63, 85, 232, 307, 342, 367, 468, 602.

**wundorlīc** *adj.* wondrous 359.

**wundorlīce** *adv.* wonderfully, *comp.* 127.

**wundrian** *wv.* 2 to marvel, wonder 331.

**wunian** *wv.* 2 to dwell, inhabit, live in 105, 172, 363, 386, 580, 609 ; to remain, exist 82, 181, 641.

**wurma** *m.* purple 294.

**wylla** *m.* well 63.

**wyllestrēam** *m.* welling waters 105, 362.

**wyllgespryng** *n.* spring, fountain 109.

**wylm** *m.* passionate desire 191 ; swell, surge 283.

**wyn** *f.* delight, joy, bliss 12, *155*, 237, 278, 290, 345, 348, 411, 480 ; **wynn** 70 ; *instr. pl.* **wynnum** joyfully, blissfully 7, 27, 313.

**wynlīc** *adj.* fair 34.

**wynlond** *n.* blissful land 82.

**wynn** *see* **wyn.**

**wynsum** *adj.* pleasant, delightful, charming 13, 65, 194, 196, 203, 245, 318, 529, 653, 659 ; *comp.* 133.

**wyrcan** *wv.* 1 to make, create, build 394, 451.

**Wyrhta** *m.* creator, maker 9, 130.

**wyrm** *m.* worm 232, 565.

**wyrt** *f.* plant, fragrant plant, spice 194, 196, 213, 265, 273, 430, 465, 474, 529, 653 ; root 172.


**yfel** *n.* evil 460, 594.

**yldo** *see* **yldu.**

**yldra** *m.* forefather 414, 438.

**yldu** *f.* old age 52, 190 ; **yldo** 614.

**ymb** *prep. w. acc.* beside, about, around 292, 305, 619 ; on account of, concerning 360, 572.

**ymbe** *prep. w. acc.* around, about 164.

**ymbfōn** *sv.* 7 to grasp 276.

**ymbhwyrft** *m.* surface, region 43.

**ymbsettan** *wv.* 1 to encompass, surround 204.

**yrfeweard** *m.* heir 376.

**yrmðu** *f.* mercy, sorrow, woe 52, 405, 614.

yrre *n.* anger, wrath 408.
ysle *f.* ash, cinder 224, 271, 286, 576.

ȳþe *adv.* easy, *superl.* 113.
ȳðaru *f.* flood, rush of waves 44.
ȳðmere *m.* billowy ocean 94.

## LATIN

Alleluia *interjection* Alleluia 677.
almus *adj.* genial ; *acc. pl. f.* (?) alma 673.
altus *adj.* high, lofty 671.
auctor *m.* creator, maker 667.
blandis *adj.* mild, gracious 674.
celum *n.* heaven, sky 669.
et *conj.* and 672, 674.
finis *m.f.* end 675.
gaudium *n.* joy, delight 669.
in *prep. w. abl.* in 669.
laus *f.* praise, glory 676.
letitia *f.* gladness ; *gen. sg.* letitię 673.

lux *f.* light 667, 672.
magnus *adj.* great, spacious, extensive ; *superl. acc. pl. n.* maxima 670.
mereor *v.* to get, obtain ; *inf.*(?) merueri 668.
mitis *adj.* mild ; *acc. sg. m.* mittem 674.
pax *f.* peace 672.
perennis *adj.* unceasing, everlasting 676.
regnum *n.* kingdom 670.
sedes *f.* seat, throne 671.
sine *prep. w. abl.* without 675.